IN THE HOLLOW
OF HIS HAND

IN THE HOLLOW OF HIS HAND

✦

The Story of Artist Arnold Stanfield

Loretta Stanfield
With
Lavada Haupt

iUniverse, Inc.
New York Lincoln Shanghai

IN THE HOLLOW OF HIS HAND
The Story of Artist Arnold Stanfield

iUniverse books may be ordered through booksellers or by contacting:

iUniverse
2021 Pine Lake Road, Suite 100
Lincoln, NE 68512
www.iuniverse.com
1-800-Authors (1-800-288-4677)

ISBN-13: 978-0-595-39577-4 (pbk)
ISBN-13: 978-0-595-83980-3 (ebk)
ISBN-10: 0-595-39577-5 (pbk)
ISBN-10: 0-595-83980-0 (ebk)

Printed in the United States of America

"He who forms the mountains, creates the wind, and reveals his thoughts to man, he who turns dawn to darkness, and treads the high places of the earth—the Lord God Almighty is his name" (Amos 4:13, NIV).

Arnold Stanfield surrendered his dream to God and then watched God perform miracles on a cold, treacherous, and void mountain.

This book is in memory of my precious husband, Arnold Stanfield, and the wonderful years God gave us together, and for all he taught me about life and how our Lord intended it to be.

Dedicated to my children:

> Frankie Proctor
> Valerie Nunnery
> Donna Bellamy

And to all the wonderful family and friends who encouraged and supported us in our endeavor to follow the Lord's will for our lives.

Contents

Introduction xiii

Foreward xv

CHAPTER 1   The Call 19

CHAPTER 2   Bending the Brushwood 23

CHAPTER 3   Where He Leads 27

CHAPTER 4   His Amazing Grace 36

CHAPTER 5   God Provides 44

CHAPTER 6   A Closer Walk with God 54

CHAPTER 7   Making Straight the Way 61

CHAPTER 8   A Time of Sorrow 66

CHAPTER 9   Home at Last 69

CHAPTER 10   Blazing Through the Nineties 71

CHAPTER 11   His Many Outlets 89

CHAPTER 12   A New Pinnacle 95

CHAPTER 13   Until We Meet Again 100

Epilogue   Memories Live On 104

Tributes 72-73, 107

Notes 115

Acknowledgements

We offer our sincere thanks to everyone who contributed in any way to this work. Thanks to friends who contributed facts, statements, and shared their love for Arnold. Without those friends, the book would not be a reality.

_____Loretta Stanfield

_____Lavada Haupt

To Barbara Brooks, who edited the material, answered questions, and searched the Internet for permission to use selected material. For her encouragement, valuable advice, and for always being accessible.

To LeDale Southerland, Lavada's neice, who edited the work, gave valuable advice, and encouragement. For her confidence in the writer of this work and for using her to share God's love and the approachability we have to Him, the Author of all.

To Kristy Dykes, who edited this project, and answered questions. For her advice, and encouragement. For her belief in the work, her enthusiasm and dedication to ensure a perfected finished work.

My special thanks to Jeff Davis, who painted three illustrations included in this book, and for his cover design. Jeff is a very busy legal artist who so graciously gave his time to do this art work for me, and I thank him so very much.

Loretta Stanfield

Introduction

Arnold Stanfield started his career as an artist by airbrushing and drawing caricatures for tourists in Gatlinburg, Tennessee. His many mediums in several states at that time included a commission of a rendering for the historic Acosta Bridge in Jacksonville, Florida.

In 1991, he opened the Stanfield Art Gallery in Cosby, Tennessee, and his prominence traveled fast. His work in many mediums became a trail of history in the mountain area he loved. He was commissioned by schools, hotels, libraries, chambers, businesses, and other entities to produce works of art, many of them historical in nature, from murals to paintings to sculptures. Many of his paintings contained a painting within a painting.

Philanthropic at heart, he donated many original pieces to organizations for their fundraising efforts. His unique art pieces generated numerous newspaper articles, commendations, and awards. Two of his original applewood art pieces, *Brotherhood of the Spirit* and *Spirit Son,* were honored by the state of Tennessee in a special ceremony in Hartford, Tennessee.

Arnold wanted people to become keenly aware of the magic of art. He desired for them to realize it was a gift from God. He believed God used his hands to show the world a small portion of the beauty of His creation.

Foreward

At the age of six, Arnold Ray Stanfield knew he wanted to paint. Even without proper materials to create paintings, he could not be outdone. With his God-given urgency to paint tugging at him, he improvised and used whatever was available, glue, sand, and food coloring to generate his first works.

One day his parents came home and were surprised to find his painting and drawing on the living room wall. They were so overwhelmed with his artistic talents and the beautiful scene, they never erased the drawing. At age 11, he won several blue ribbons at the Georgia State Fair for his work.

His small stature did not stop him. He had beaten all the odds when he was born in Brunswick, Georgia as a blue baby in 1940. Without today's medical technology, he was sent home to die. Because of the love and determination of his mother, the two-pound baby boy developed and flourished, though he was 12 years old before his size and weight closely equaled other children his age.

Throughout his school years, his teachers were a blessing in disguise. They assigned him special art projects that gave him painting experience. He was truly creative, and I believe God put him on earth as a creative being.

God led him in many ways. For instance, when he was in the Navy, he was deployed at sea when an engine on the ship broke.

The crew would have to stay in the middle of the ocean another two months waiting for the part needed to repair the engine.

Arnold asked his captain if he could try and fix it. The captain told him he couldn't do it. Arnold believed he could and convinced him it wouldn't hurt to try. Arnold repaired the engine, fired it up, and brought them back home. For this service, he received a special award from the military. After his death, I received a certificate of commendation from The President of the United States for Arnold's service to his country when he repaired the engine.

When Arnold was discharged from the Navy, he free-handed the state draftsman test for the state of Georgia. He passed the test with flying colors, and the state put him to work. He didn't have the experience or the education in that field. He, however, decided to take civil engineering correspondence courses. He did so well he earned his engineering technician degree. He worked for several large civil engineering companies until 1980 when he went into full-time art work.

Arnold and I met in 1977 while attending the singles Sunday school class at First Baptist Church in Jacksonville, Florida. Jeannie and Joe Vaughn introduced us.

A few months before our September 2, 1977 marriage, Arnold told me he felt God calling him into full-time painting. He asked me if I would be willing for him to do that, and if I would move to the Smoky Mountains with him. I was so in love, I promised him I would go with him, not realizing at first I would be leaving my three children, Frankie 20, Valerie 17, and Donna 16 for the first time in their lives.

Two years later, Arnold and I moved to Tennessee. It was a difficult separation from my children and parents, but God filled the gap for me and gave me blessings beyond anything I could have ever expected.

Loretta Stanfield

1

The Call

"God is calling me into full-time painting," Arnold Stanfield told Loretta. "In the mountains of Tennessee. Our lives will transcend back to pioneering days, struggles, hardships, and destitution such as you've never imagined."

Yet his bride of almost two years, Loretta Proctor Stanfield, gladly followed him into their new land of vast enormity—the unknown—their milk and honey ordained by God.

"It is God who arms me with strength and makes my way perfect. He makes my feet like the feet of a deer; he enables me to stand on the heights. He trains my hands for battle; my arms can bend a bow of bronze. You give me your shield of victory, and your right hand sustains me; you stoop down to make me great. You broaden the path beneath me, so that my ankles do not turn" (Psalm 18:32-36, NIV).

At the age of 37, Arnold Stanfield, a civil engineer in Jacksonville, Florida, started down the path to accomplish the dream and calling from God he'd had since he was six years old. Knowing it was God's plan for this time in his life, he didn't hesitate to accept His call and go into full-time painting. God was sending him, and he knew His promises were true. God would be by his side.

Arnold trusted God to give him strength and make his way perfect. Just as God sent Moses a helpmate, he sent Loretta Proctor to Arnold...

Love quickly blossomed for Arnold and Loretta. However, Loretta did a little holding out. She said no the first time he asked her to marry him. Arnold persisted. He asked her a second time one Tuesday night at a church visitation dinner—in front of 1,000 people!

"I didn't give him an answer," Loretta said. "I was too stunned."

Not to be outdone, Arnold called her two weeks before Labor Day. "What are you doing Labor Day weekend?" he asked.

"I haven't made any plans yet," she promptly replied.

"Good," he said. "That will give us a three-day honeymoon."

"Oh! Yes." She answered without hesitation this time. She had been so in love with him all along, but trepidation had gnawed at her. She had prayed, then prayed some more, and this time when he asked, there were no doubts in her heart. She knew this was what God would have her do.

Arnold told her to call her best friends, Faye and Bill Luper, and ask if she and Arnold could get married in their home and if Faye would handle the reception. He told Loretta to tell her they would pay all the costs. He said they could get the older gentleman, a minister and pastor of a church on U.S. 1 in Jacksonville, to perform the wedding ceremony. The minister was also a dear friend of Loretta's.

"He had everything planned out, so I couldn't say no," Loretta said. "So that's what we did."

Then Arnold told Loretta of his plans for the future. "I love you and want to marry you," he told her, "but God is sending me into a world that will change our lives." Arnold had visited the Smoky Mountains many times and felt God calling him there. Each time he visited and searched for a place to live, he had no doubt God would lead him to the exact place He wanted him and Loretta to live.

"I'll go with you," she quickly replied.

Almost two years after their marriage, he took another journey of faith. He went on a short, fact-finding mission to the Smoky Mountains one weekend, looking for the place God had predestined for him and his wife. With his stepson by his side, he found eight acres for $600 on Short Mountain in Cosby, Tennessee. The mountain was peaked, but Arnold had no doubt that God would help him flatten the peak so he could build a home. He returned home and told Loretta he had bought her a mountain.

In October 1979, while they were on vacation, Arnold took his wife up that narrow, rugged, one-way lane. When he reached the end of the lane, his face glowed. He showed her their eight acres of land. At that time, the lane leading to the top of the mountain was nothing more than a forest of trees and underbrush. He could not contain his enthusiasm. His eyes shone as bright as stars on a dark night. He had come home, to his mountain situated between two slightly higher mountains.

They returned from vacation, and Arnold was encouraged by Loretta's determination and desire to follow God's will. On December 30, he gave his notice for his civil engineering job.

Arnold didn't have a doubt that the years ahead would be long and hard, and at times almost unbearable. It was only through the power of God that he could come to terms with leaving the security of his job and take his wife away from all she'd been accustomed to in the big city.

Sometimes Satan's attacks would be stronger than others. Maybe, Arnold thought, because he didn't pray hard enough. He was asking Loretta to leave her family and go with him to an undeveloped mountain. God would remind him that he had given Loretta a choice, and that without hesitation, she was willing to make that sacrifice to be with him.

The call from God was so strong and compelling that each time doubts rose in his mind, Arnold prayed harder, asking God to remove those doubts. He asked God to remove any skepticism or fear, and to fill him with assurance that God, himself, was leading him into this new and strange life.

"Lord, I'm going on faith," he prayed. "I'm trusting You that through all the hardships Loretta and I will face, You will strengthen us and make straight our path so that in the end, we will have accomplished Your will. Let my life, my new birth through Your Son, Jesus, be an example to those faltering by the wayside. Let others come to know and trust You as Savior."

Arnold went forward, never looking back, knowing that all his help would come from God.

2

Bending the Brushwood

Arnold loaded up the family Ford Bronco on February 1, 1980, and headed for the mountain property alone to build a place for him and his wife. That was strong motivation for him because he didn't want Loretta to come until he had a place for her to stay.

He drove through Cosby, Tennessee, and to the lane that led to their future home. He passed several lanes leading into mountainous areas, but he followed the curvaceous trail to the bottom of Short Mountain. The adjacent property to his right had not yet been developed. When he reached the mountain, the only trail to follow was the old 50-foot overgrown trail that curved to his left and stopped at the bottom of an approximately 100-foot incline.

It seemed the trail, at one time, extended a few feet further, but the whole area had not been traveled for years. It had become overgrown with small trees, mountain laurel, and other shrub and undergrowth. The lane was totally impassable, and the incline to his left too steep to drive his Bronco. He parked at the foot of the incline. As he had done before when he assessed the area, he walked up the incline and crossed over the steep rugged trail that led to the peak of Short Mountain.

Again, he surveyed the small piece of property that fit between the mountainside and trail. He calculated that the small area where the land did not seem so steep was about an eighth of a mile long. His plans to flatten the land and build a temporary home energized him although he was fully aware that it would take some time to build a drivable road to the top of the mountain.

He realized the monstrosity of the task that lay before him. It would take many long hours of hard work to prepare the lower land. He needed to clear and flatten it so he could build a temporary home while he worked on edging his way to their future destination and homestead. He stood on the trail and looked up toward the mountain peak, knowing that the craggy path trailed to the open space in the sky. He knew that even with a bulldozer, it would not be easy to engineer a drivable road that reached toward heaven.

He walked farther up the rugged, steep path. A fourth of a mile later, he came to a slingback to the left—a sharp turn that paralleled the trail. The path, however, continued on a steep incline.

Arnold reached the end of the trail and stood at the edge of the drop off. If someone drove off the edge, it would lead to almost certain death. When the lane was widened, a driver would have to keep his vehicle moving. If he stopped on the curve, he would have no choice but to back down the trail.

It was a dangerous, threatening ride that only the most seasoned drivers would dare attempt. A sharp right turn seemed to climb into the sky. To his left, the path ended and dropped to a mountainside covered with foliage, trees, and underbrush. Arnold drew a deep breath as he looked about and saw the beauty of God's creation, and he had not even reached the top.

It was time to move on, higher into the sky, nearer the heavens, to where God was leading him.

Air pulled from his lungs as he struggled over the rugged path—higher—higher. At last, he reached the peak. As he looked about, his first observation was confirmed. The mountain could be leveled off to a flat surface. He could build a home high in the sky and paint while living at the tip of the beautiful mountain terrain. But being a civil engineer, he knew it would take time and tremendous effort.

First, he would have to get started on a temporary home. Bringing Loretta to the mountain was imperative. He missed her already. He looked down and stared at the mountain forest. It would take years to build a permanent home.

In the meantime and while he prepared a temporary home, he wanted to paint. He would do that which God had called him to do from this glorious view. He remembered Deuteronomy 31:23 where God told Joshua to be strong and of good courage and that He would be with him. Arnold knew this message was also true and relevant for him.

When he returned to the bottom of the mountain, he set up camp. It was not the usual campsite that campers are accustomed to. During his earlier trips to the mountain, he knew he'd have to set up a crude campsite for several weeks. In preparation, he cut down four trees and made posts. He dug holes in the ground and secured the posts. Then he took an old blue tarp and hung it over them as a cover for his rugged campsite.

Arnold opened a lounge chair for his bed. He put a small chair at the end of the lounge chair, and on that he placed his flashlight and a picture of Loretta.

Exhausted, he bowed his head and thanked God for bringing him to this place and for giving him his meager camp. Then he settled down on his chaise lounge, smiling at the picture of his wife. With a contented long sigh, he closed his eyes.

God, however, had more testing for Arnold Stanfield that night. It was about 2 a. m. when thunder rolled onto his campsite. Lightning flashed around him, and the wind and rain swirled against his tarp, toppling it within minutes. With rain soaking through his clothes, he grabbed Loretta's picture and his flashlight and crawled into his Bronco.

He remembered an old schoolhouse and a streetlight a short distance down that long twisting road. He told Loretta later that he'd never been so happy to see a streetlight. He parked beneath it, moved into the back, and slept the rest of the night.

For two weeks, he slept in his Bronco beside the schoolhouse even though he couldn't stretch out.

3

Where He Leads

Arnold knew the only way to experience power from God was to pray. And that's what he did as he faced many obstacles to reach his goal and become an artist. He knew that through the power of God, he could do what God had called him to do. He remembered a verse he'd learned years ago. "Show me your ways, O Lord, teach me your paths; guide me in your truth and teach me, for you are God my Savior, and my hope is in you all day long" (Psalm 25:4-5, NIV).

Arnold wanted his work to awaken the minds of those who studied his art. He wanted them to see a deeper meaning, to see that each stroke of his brush was ordained by God. It was his goal that everyone who saw his art would understand and accept God's strength and leadership in their lives. He strove for excellence in pointing others to know the wonderful, magical God and His calling in their lives.

He wanted people to know that God calls each of His children to serve Him in whatever capacity He has given them. Arnold's dream was to awaken the sleeping giant within the hearts of those who saw his work.

Arnold worked vigorously to clear an area on the old trail at the top of the 100-foot incline. The trail abutted the 50-foot incline where he planned to build a temporary cabin. He bent the brush-wood that covered the ground, using his ax, hoe, shovel, and hacksaw. He cut down many trees and underbrush, including the spreading mountain laurel bush, and dug out roots. Each time he felled a tree or pulled a bush, it shortened the time when his wife could join him on the mountain.

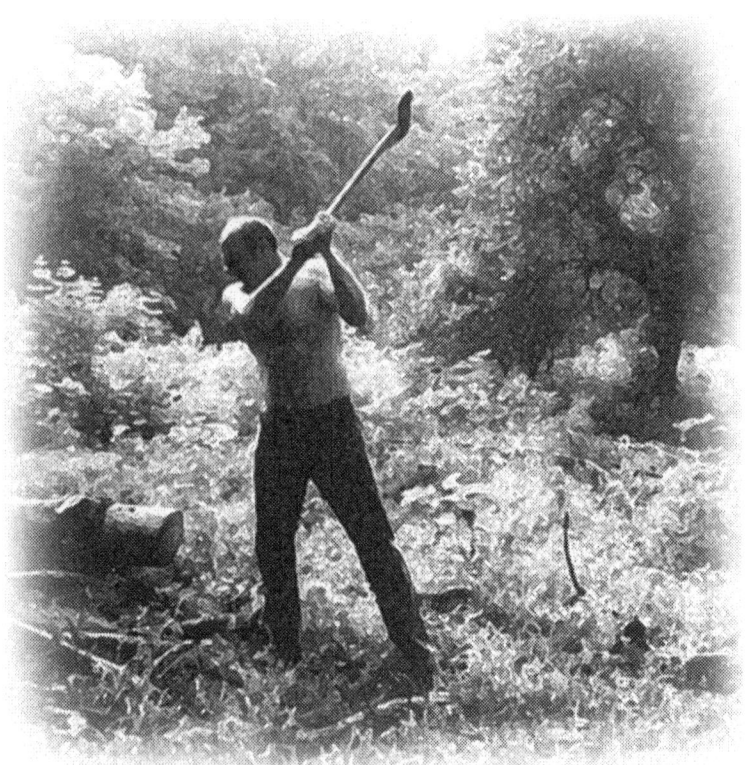

Arnold at work clearing the mountain property.

Although it was cold, Arnold sweated, sometimes having to shed his outer coat because of the exhaustive heat building up and pouring from his body. Finally, he cleared enough space and leveled enough ground in a small area to set up camp.

The spot was rugged, still needing much work. However, two weeks after he arrived on the mountain, Loretta's son, Frankie, and Arnold's nephew, Bob, told him they could not stand her moaning and groaning anymore.

With their home in Jacksonville up for sale, Arnold consented for Loretta to move up with him, but with one condition. They'd have to bring a small tent-top, pop-up camper for him and Loretta to live in while he built their temporary home. Although he had asked that one of the men drive his old van to Tennessee when they came, he knew that with no heat in the van and a leak in the roof, it would not provide safe and adequate sleeping quarters for Loretta.

Arnold was already laying the groundwork to build their cabin. He needed a home with enough room to set up a shop where he could paint. He was prodded on by a sense of urgency in his heart, a constant reminder that God had called him to use the gift He had given him. Arnold's plan was to make every minute count and complete the task before him so he could open a shop.

When Loretta, her son, and Arnold's nephew arrived on Short Mountain in mid-February 1980, it was a happy reunion. Sleeping quarters were sparse, however, so the two men slept in Arnold's van or in their cars parked near Arnold and Loretta's camper.

While the men were there, they went up the 50-foot incline that adjoined the trail from the left. It was a rugged, steep piece of land that snuggled against the bottom of the mountain.

Arnold knew it was the only area where he could build a tempo-rary home, so he and the men shoveled out a large area on the side of the mountain.

They continued to work until they had widened, lengthened, and flattened the area Arnold had already begun to clear. They also wanted to make sure that the old overgrown trail was large enough for the camper. A forest of mostly smaller trees and underbrush covered the trail. It was the same trail Arnold had walked on to the top of the mountain. They cut down small trees and pulled roots from the path. With the trees, they made a large flat square for Arnold to place the camper.

Time ran out. The men had to go back to Florida on Mon-day so they could report for work Tuesday morning. Arnold assured them he would somehow manage to move the camper to the cleared area on the path at the top of the incline.

After the men left, Arnold continued shoveling and clearing the area. In the meantime, he and Loretta lived in the camper still parked in the middle of the county road at the bottom of the 100-foot incline.

A week later, Arnold decided it was time to pull the camper to the top of the 100-foot incline to the path on their property. However, that was a colossal drawback for Arnold. How could he pull the camper up the incline to the trail and to the small area he and the men had prepared?

It was all uphill, and the only spot flat enough to cross over was an area covered over with a run-off stream. It was just a continuous running spring that perhaps had been there for years, but the water had made a patch of mud too deep to pull the camper through.

He knew it was dangerous to pull the camper up the hill by himself. He debated the situation with Loretta. Although determined and courageous, it was only after much prayer that he agreed to let Loretta help him. However, he would not let Loretta get behind the camper in case it started rolling backward. All he allowed her to do was pull while he pushed.

They had it almost to the top when Arnold lost his hold on it.

Loretta looked down at her husband, knowing he could be seriously hurt if it rolled back on him. "God gave me extraordinary strength," Loretta said, "and I was able to hold it off him until he could gain control again."

Arnold stood the camper on end and dog-walked it the rest of the way. Although the taillights had busted out, they had a camper to sleep in that night. And it was on their own property.

During the days that followed, Arnold worked tirelessly to saw or chop down the sea of trees and dig up roots. He pulled up the underlying brush and shrubbery that seemed to have no end.

Every morning he would trudge up the 50-foot incline and clear an area that would eventually be a 250-foot-long strip that tapered off into the trail leading up the mountain. The width was 150 feet wide and abutted the trail. The western end of the space abutted the edge of the mountain foliage and trees, with too sharp a drop to level any further.

In March, 1980, Arnold started building one room of the cabin. With their money depleted, and satisfied he had done all he could without more funds, he went into Gatlinburg to look for work. The vacation town was 27 miles west and a 45-minute drive on the curvaceous mountain roads. All he could find was work as a caricaturist. Knowing they needed the money for food and supplies to make their mountain more livable, he took whatever job he could get.

Arnold would not allow Loretta to stay on the mountain alone, so he took her with him every day because it was too dangerous to leave her. He worried about wild animals such as panthers, wildcats, and bears that sometimes traveled along the county road. And if a wind kicked up strong enough and beat against their camper, it could knock it off the mountain.

Every morning, they worked on their property and cabin. Then they'd go into Gatlinburg about noon, in time for the tourist businesses to open.

Sometimes Loretta read, but when needed, she worked for the young girl who managed the Dairy Queen in the same mall where Arnold painted caricatures. She later became one of Loretta's good friends.

The caricatures were cartoons or comic strips that tourists in Gatlinburg wanted. Arnold was a natural at airbrush, so whatever they asked for, he would paint. He loved drawing the caricatures, and he was delighted when he saw pleasure and happy smiles on the faces of the tourists when he finished a drawing.

Arnold and Loretta's time together was spent working and driving into town. When they returned home at night, he spent every minute working on the cabin. Loretta stayed by his side, helping him every way she could.

Arnold cut wood to burn so he could keep a fire going outside for warmth. He put a two-burner Coleman oil stove on a picnic table just outside the cabin for Loretta to cook on—that is if they had food to cook.

Loretta now smiles at that memory. "I lost 20 pounds the first month we lived up there, and he lost about 30 pounds."

Times were hard, so they ate mostly bologna sandwiches. However, if possible, when they felt the need to have a change in diet, they'd buy a jar of peanut butter. They kept a loaf of bread all the time, and they kept one-half gallon of milk in the cold water of Bailey Branch, a little branch that runs all the way through the hollow and into the Cosby Creek.

At least once a week, they bought a chicken and a vegetable. Sometimes, Arnold would build a big wood fire and Loretta would cook on that.

Loretta still remembers the thrill when a neighbor came up that narrow trail to their camp. "They'd often bring us a jar of homemade jelly," she said. "Oh, how good that was."

Soon after they moved to the mountain, Arnold found an old refrigerator rack and a liquor still that perhaps had been used in illegal moonshine operations years ago. He put them together and used large rocks to build an Indian pit. He put the old liquor steel pipe over it so they could have heat and fire to cook on.

"We had to keep the stove outside," Loretta said, "but even so, it gave off a lot of heat, making it a good heater in the morning and at night."

Arnold found an old metal rack at the dumpster and took it home. He covered it with aluminum foil and placed it on the Indian-type cookstove he had made with rocks.

Not only was the food delicious to them but to others as well. A professor from the University of Tennessee in Knoxville had also bought property in that area. "He and his wife lived in an 80-year-old cabin farther back from us," Loretta said. "When they came to the mountain, they often stopped and told us how good the food smelled," Loretta said.

Wanting to be good neighbors, Arnold and Loretta invited the professor and his wife to have dinner with them whenever they could. The professor told them it was the best food he ever tasted.

Later, Arnold discovered he could put red hot coals in a hot dog cooker and put the cooker on the floor of the camper for heat. "Of course," Loretta said, "we had to be very careful because it was dangerous, so we constantly supervised it."

Arnold and Loretta lived without modern conveniences. In fact, it was less than bare necessities. They didn't have electricity, phone, or running water. They took their water containers down to the closest neighbor, and they'd let them get water.

Bathing was an unmerciful challenge. They left camp early on their way to town and stopped at the river to take a bath. It was springtime and the water, covered with ice and snow, flowed from the frozen mountain top. Loretta vividly remembers the icy water and its piercing sting.

"You can be sure there were no germs left on us," she said.

4

His Amazing Grace

Danger was everywhere, but God's grace was real. Their Heavenly Father showered them with His protection during the next 12 months. Arnold continued to put his trust in God, praying and seeking God's guidance. As he prayed and trusted God, so did Loretta. They both learned a new meaning of trusting God, thankful for the times they had to read and study God's Word.

This was not a forced way of life for Arnold and Loretta. This was their chosen way of life because Arnold was following God's leadership. Loretta understood this and accepted the fact that Arnold was being obedient to God. Arnold's way of life was her way, and she wanted to follow him wherever God led him. It was a good life because they were together doing what God wanted them to do. "I knew that for Arnold to be successful, I had to be willing to follow him as God led him. I knew that all our hardships would fade and we'd remember only the good."

When neighbors heard they were living in the hollow, they rode back there to make sure it was true. The hollow was an unused, overgrown area that was dark, cold, and damp. It was like a long, deep cavity going through an undeveloped area.

The hollow begins at the dirt road that leads off the main road, and it's the only trail that leads to the mountain. The hollow is the whole area that leads back to the foot of the mountain, past where Arnold and Loretta first camped, and it circles around behind the mountain. They never traveled to the end of the hollow.

"After we moved to the hollow, many people stopped and introduced themselves," Loretta said. "Many were concerned that we lived so far back away from everyone."

Jimmy Breedon, a neighbor who lived about a mile away, asked Arnold to consider moving into his garage apartment until they built their cabin because it was so dangerous and cold in the hollow. Others came and asked them to move to different places for safety, but they stayed in the hollow. "Being the man Arnold was," Loretta said, "he trusted and expected God to watch over us."

"The mountains loomed up on both sides and behind us," Loretta said. "The sun could sneak in for only a couple of hours in the afternoon." There was hardly any warmth from the sun, and they were cold most of the time. Ice and snow did not melt fast in the hollow because it was veiled from the warmth of the sun.

"It was amazing how much the people accepted and welcomed us," Loretta said. The people were close-knit and protective of each other. They did not always accept strangers, but they were kind neighbors from the beginning. One person told them it was because they did not try to change them. Arnold and Loretta accepted them as they were and received them as family and friends.

On April 15, 1980, income tax day, it was 15 degrees. It was too cold to stay in the camper with no heat, so Arnold and Loretta stayed in their old van. They'd made the back of the van into a small camper, and they would crank it every so often and get a little warm. "We stayed under blankets, but we were still very cold."

When they went to the post office to mail their taxes, the postmistress recognized that they were new in the area. She asked their names and if they were Christians. They told her they were, and she wanted to know if they were living there permanently. They said yes, and she invited them to attend the revival service at her church the next night.

Arnold and Loretta were excited about going to the services just to be in a warm building and with Christian people. They enjoyed meeting everyone at the small Union Missionary Baptist Church. As it turned out, they went to the revival every night.

Loretta discovered she had a problem. When she'd packed before leaving Jacksonville, she had only enough room for one dress. "That was an adjustment," Loretta said, "because I had to wear the same dress every night and then on Sunday. Arnold had one pair of dress slacks and a shirt. But no one seemed to notice our wardrobe selection. It was a joy for us to be with our new Christian friends."

Myrtle Breeden, one of the older ladies and Jimmy Breeden's mother, asked Loretta if she'd like to go to her house for a warm tub bath. Of course, Loretta could hardly wait. That's when she learned to love Mrs. Breeden, a godly woman who became like a mother to her.

Loretta started taking her everywhere. At least once a month, while Arnold worked on building their cabin, she went down the mountain and made homemade pie crusts for her new friend who'd lived in the same house all of her life.

Arnold had not yet been able to get water to their mountain, so Mrs. Breeden provided water from her well. Many times she would cook for them. Arnold and Loretta's pastor, the Reverend Randall as they called him, found out they were living back in the hollow and often visited them.

Arnold sent Loretta back to Jacksonville to sell their home after the contracts with two realtors expired. He wanted Loretta to put it on the market. She sold it within two weeks.

While she was gone, the temperature dropped to 15 degrees again. Arnold was alone and colder than he had ever been. He went up the mountain, chopped down trees, chained them together, and dragged them down the mountain.

He'd found several iron bars, and he drove them into the ground. Then he skinned the trees with a square shovel, notched them with the chain saw, and stacked them against the iron bars to keep them from rolling down the incline. When he had enough logs, he stacked them around the space he'd cleared for the cabin.

"No one ever worked so hard to build a cabin as Arnold did," Loretta said. "Years ago," Loretta said, "neighbors and friends would have a cabin or barn raising. Within a short time, the building would be complete. But Arnold had no one to help him."

Working alone did not discourage him because he knew it was impossible to have a cabin raising in the area. However, many came and helped him a few hours at a time. Even their pastor helped when he had time. However, if they were not used to the work, they could not last long.

While Loretta was in Jacksonville, Arnold's brother came up to help him. Arnold told him he could sleep in his old van parked at the bottom of the drive. Before Loretta left, she had made Arnold promise to check the camper each night and make sure nothing was in there that should not be. The first night his brother was there, Arnold lifted his pillow and found the largest black snake he'd ever seen.

The snake went out the back underneath the canvas on the camper, and Arnold went out the front door. He ran down to the van and told his brother to move over. The camper was not big enough for him and the snake.

One morning after Loretta returned, the temperature dropped to 15 degrees yet again. To make matters worse, it was raining. "We had never been so horribly cold," Loretta said. "We piled all our clothes and all the covers we had on top of us."

Arnold didn't think he could build a fire in the cold, damp mountain, but he got up anyway to try.

"I heard him out there doing everything possible to start a fire," Loretta said.

Finally, he came back in and prayed. "Lord, if You want us to have a fire You'll have to build it because I can't." He settled back in bed, then sat up again. "Do you hear that?"

Loretta stirred under the weight of the covers. "Hear what?"

"I believe the Lord has built us a fire. I hear something crackling out there."

Arnold so completely trusted God that Loretta was not surprised when he got up and looked outside. "Sure enough," she said, "a fire had started in our rock fireplace, an inglenook he'd built right outside our camper to keep coals and fire from the woods. We both started praising God."

Days passed, and they still had to climb the 50-foot incline every time they went to the top of their property to work. The van was still parked on the county road at the bottom of the 100-foot incline. Arnold was anxious to move it up to the path where they were camped.

About a week later, after cutting down small trees and clearing a roadway, he was ready to move the van to the path. Once the van was near their camp, they could propel it to the top of the 50-foot incline.

It was on a Sunday morning, and Loretta was in the camper dressing for church when Arnold came up the hill.

"I need you to help me," he said, a sheepish grin spreading across his face.

"I knew he was up to something," she said, "or had done something he shouldn't have. I raised my eyebrows and waited for him to tell me what he wanted.

"I need you to go with me and get in the van."

"Where's the van?"

He hesitated then told her he'd driven it up on the hill. He had tried to turn it around to drive back down around the curve. He realized he could not turn around, neither could he back up."

"I'm headed straight for the cliff through some trees," he said. "I'll topple over the cliff if I can't turn around and aim it down the hill."

Loretta knew there was only one option. She had to get in the van, and he had to get in the Bronco and snatch the van off the cliff. He attached a chain from the Bronco to the front of the van. After he assured Loretta she'd be safe, she agreed to get in the van and hold the brake down as hard as she could. She was to let up on it when he gave the signal.

Loretta held the brake down but she was scared. "He signaled and pressed down on the gas pedal of the Bronco. Nothing happened. He told me we'd try again, and we did. Still, the van did not move. Before the third try, I looked down and realized my foot was glued to the brake, so I let up on it when he signaled me the third time."

Arnold jerked the van completely off the cliff. He kept going, knocking down trees in their path, until he went off the hill.

"It sounds dangerous," Loretta said, "but Arnold knew what he was doing. Although I was nervous, I had to remember that Arnold had never lied to me or put me in a dangerous situation. I relaxed and felt completely confident in his judgment."

Arnold looked perplexed as he hurried to her. "I can't figure why it took three times for me to get the van off there."

"He looked at me," Loretta said, "and knew I had been holding the brake down. I gave a nervous laugh and in a tiny voice said I'd never do that again."

The next day Arnold decided to try again to drive the van off the county road to their property. The curve was on a hill, and he had almost reached the bottom when the van skidded. He ended up dangling from the side of the hill, half of the van on the ground, the other half suspended in the air.

"I was standing to the side," Loretta said, "and, of course, as I did almost daily, I prayed, *Lord it's us again and we are in trouble again. Please send someone to help us get this van off the mountain.*

As soon as Loretta finished praying, a big old woods truck with a long flat bed stopped in front of them. "An inebriated elderly man climbed out of the truck," Loretta said. "Another older man got out of the passenger side."

The driver told Arnold to get back in the van and hold on. He warned him that he'd come down real hard, but he'd keep going until Arnold was ready to drive the van back around on flat ground. Then he chained his truck to the van and snatched it off the mountain into the field.

Arnold held onto the wheel with an iron grip. The van did just what the man said it would. It soared down the cliff and landed upright, then continued across the fields until the man could slow down and stop.

They thanked the stranger and praised the Lord again. God had used someone under the influence of alcohol to help accomplish His will for them. Although amazed, they were reminded that God loves everyone regardless of the situation.

Every day, they saw how God's hand was in what they were doing. Arnold knew that his step of faith pleased God. God had made moving to the mountains a reality, and Arnold knew he could trust God to take care of them now. He had no doubt God would honor his and Loretta's efforts to obey Him as they struggled through hardships.

"Remember this is something we chose to do," Loretta said, "not something we had to do. God took care of us even when we put Him to the test over and over."

It was not an easy life, and every day Arnold labored to complete their temporary home. Time, it seemed, was passing fast. His heart and mind were crying to create through art.

5

God Provides

The spring water was causing deep mud all the way across their drive, and as a civil engineer, Arnold knew he needed to drain the water. However, he could not afford a culvert, the one thing necessary to make his drive passable and bring him a step closer to painting. He remembered a verse he often quoted. "Not that we are competent in ourselves to claim anything for ourselves, but our competence comes from God" (2 Corinthians 3:5, NIV).

Defeat was not even a consideration for Arnold. He trusted God's promises. A few days later as he and Loretta drove into Gatlinburg one morning, he pointed toward a pile of debris off the road. "Look at that trash dump. That's just what I need."

It was a piece of culvert that the state had thrown away because one end of it was bent. It was useless to the state in that condition, but not to Arnold. "I'm going to take that home and use it on our drive where the water is running through."

Loretta was not accustomed to gathering anything out of the garbage dump. "We don't have any way to get it to our property," she said, using the best defense she could think of at the time.

He wasn't deterred. He knew he needed it and why. It was not trash to him. Before Loretta knew what was happening, he was putting it in the back of their van. "We took it home that night after work," she said.

Arnold spent the following day digging a tunnel by hand. He put the culvert in place. Again, using his hands, he covered it up.

"That was a good day for me," Loretta said, "because I spent most of it reading and studying God's Word." With a touch of nostalgia, she said, "Oh, every day was a good day, but seldom could either one of us spend a whole day reading and studying God's Word."

Arnold learned to lean on God and trust Him more every day. At night he'd build a bonfire, and he and Loretta would sit and talk, laugh, and share the memories of the past, the goodness of God, their dreams of the future, and Arnold's painting.

Whenever possible, they'd take long walks up the mountain. "One day," Loretta said, "we had planned a short walk, but it is easy to get lost in the mountains, especially if it's all new territory. There are so many hills and curves."

"I know where we have to go so we can get back to our property," Arnold said.

But Loretta wasn't sure he knew how to get back. "It took us almost all day to get home. We had not taken anything to drink or eat. When we finally arrived home, we realized that we had only one can of beans. I didn't usually care for beans, but they tasted good that day."

Arnold also took Loretta for a short walk every day. However, there was a spot back in the hollow they had not walked on. In fact, they had not seen it. One day, they walked along the side of Bailey Branch and discovered they had entered a cave.

There was nothing but the little creek on one side and the mountain on the other.

"We ended up way back in an opening where there was an old cabin, and the inside was lined with newspapers. The cabin and newspapers were about 100 years old. We later learned that it had been about 30 years since anyone had lived back there. The old couple who had lived in the cabin had died."

Arnold wanted to climb every mountain and hill in the hollow. One day they were climbing a side of the mountain and came to a log. Arnold always protected Loretta and made sure she was not in danger or frightened. But as they crawled along on their hands and knees because the mountain was too steep to walk up, he couldn't stop her from an unexpected fear.

"We came to a log, and I grasped it so I could climb on up." Terror seized her when she put her hand on a soft furry object that moved. "I screamed until I saw it was a chipmunk."

Arnold took this opportunity to do something special for Loretta. "When we returned home, he airbrushed a chipmunk scampering away on a T-shirt for me. I was thrilled because it was a lovely reminder of the thrills and excitement in our pioneering life.

"It was a kindness from him I had learned to expect, an expression of gratitude for our togetherness as we explored our new surroundings and God's beautiful creations. Although the way we had chosen was a struggle, our hearts flourished with love as we witnessed the new dawning of each day and felt God drawing us nearer to Him."

Arnold loved to have Loretta by his side. Although she couldn't do the work he did, she stayed close by, doing what she could. She discovered what it was to get dirty. She had always wanted to be perfectly groomed, so when dirt covered her,

Arnold playfully laughed and teased her. "We don't have to worry about ants or ticks," he would tell her. "You killed them all by pouring out dishwater you loaded with Clorox to kill germs."

"He was full of laughter and easygoing," Loretta said. "He was funny and his good humor lightened our life and brought us an ever-constant happiness."

Arnold worked hard to develop friends in the area, and he thanked God every day for those lasting friendships. He would pray with Loretta, thanking God for the true joy He had given them. During all this time, the Lord truly protected and kept them safe. All of this increased Arnold's desire to paint and to use his God-given talent.

His perseverance paid off. In March, 1980, he started building the kitchen for their temporary cabin. Arnold didn't dig a basement for the cabin because it was imperative that he and Loretta have a safe, secure place to live as quickly as possible. Therefore, he poured a slab of concrete for the one-room foundation. (Later, he poured a concrete slab for each room as he built it.)

"Of course, we didn't have water," Loretta said, "so I hauled water up the hill for him to mix the concrete. The flow of water from the small spring was steady, but it was not enough for Arnold to mix a large amount of concrete."

Although the cabin was a superstructure, all above ground, as an engineer, he knew how important it was for all the parts of the building to fit together if he and Loretta were to have a safe abode.

He knew all the construction terms. For instance, words such as dead load, girders, columns, joists, and beams were familiar to him. He cut and measured precisely, never willing to take a shortcut regardless of how much time he could save. He knew the precise consistency necessary to make the concrete safe. Every aspect had to be exact.

He took the cabinets out of the van and fitted them into the one-room structure. Throughout the summer and early fall, he worked tirelessly until he had built a tight, secure room.

Arnold's brother went to Georgia and retrieved an old sink that his and Arnold's parents used when they started housekeeping. Arnold and Loretta bought a cookstove, sink, small table and two chairs, small refrigerator, and a single three-quarter bed and put them in the one room cabin.

In October, 1980, Arnold and Loretta moved into their one-room cabin. It was their kitchen, living room, and bedroom. Loretta could sit on the bed and turn on a burner on the stove.

The electric company strung wire across the mountainside so they could have electricity. However, for two months, until electric poles were put in, they used the stove for heat. Electricity had never been put in the hollow, so the company returned with dynamite and blasted through the rock to put in power poles.

"The cabin was warm, cozy, and oh, what victory and praise we had," Loretta said.

In February, 1981, Arnold finished a small sitting room, and he took the last forty dollars they had at the time and went into town and bought materials to build a fireplace in the sitting room. Arnold seemed to swell with new energy and zest to complete the cabin because his next step would be to build a workshop where he could paint.

He and Loretta rejoiced at what they had already done. Arnold had given his sweat, his whole being into building that cabin, but he wanted it completed. God's calling him to paint nudged harder, and he could visualize the shop he had already designed in his mind.

Knowing that he was weak within himself, that all his strength came from God, Arnold placed his confidence in God's promises. "For the eyes of the Lord range throughout the earth to strengthen those whose hearts are fully committed to him" (2 Chronicles 16:9a, NIV). As Arnold struggled with the harshness of life in the hollow, he felt closer to God and depended on Him to fulfill the dream he and Loretta shared for their lives.

Using his every ounce of strength and fortitude, Arnold worked many hours each day. His dream further unfolded when in July, 1981, he added a bedroom to the cabin. A year later, he completed the cabin.

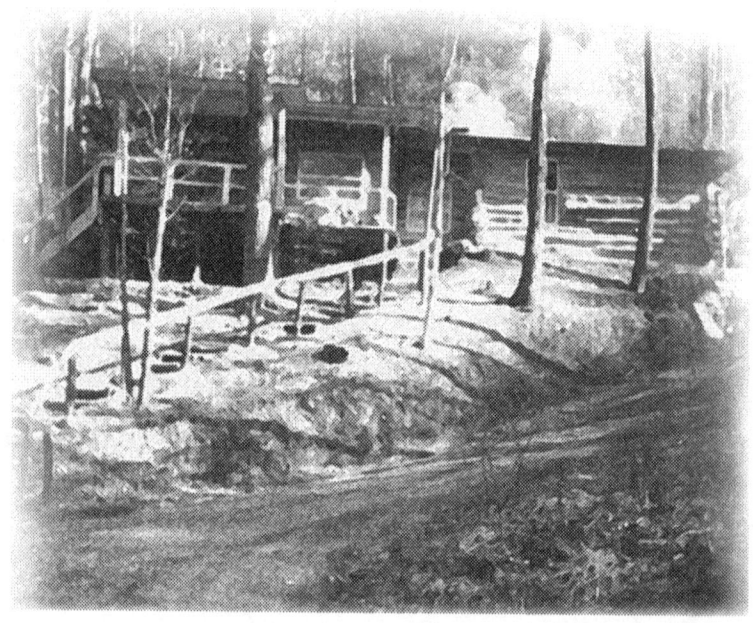

The completed temporary cabin at the bottom of the mountain
in the hollow. It sets between the base of the mountain and the
path leading to the top of the mountain.

"During the time after we spent our last forty dollars," Loretta said, "we lived off the money Arnold earned airbrushing."

Arnold wanted Loretta to spend time with her family, so they invited her parents to come spend a few days with them.

"No, thank you," her mother promptly said. She told Loretta she had taken leave of her senses or that Arnold had brainwashed her. She missed her daughter, though, and wanted to spend time with her. She told Arnold that she'd consider visiting as soon as he built a real bathroom. She had no intentions of using their outdoor one.

Arnold's mother visited, but at first she caused Loretta to feel sorry for herself because of the way they were living. "I had to do a lot of praying after she left, but she was the only one who would come up and stay with us and live the rugged lifestyle we lived. Her willingness to live our lifestyle filled me with a new respect for her."

Arnold discovered over and over the kindness of their neighbors. They always asked Arnold and Loretta if there was anything they needed. Members of their church would give them fresh vegetables, fruits, and lots of jelly from every fruit imaginable.

"After that first initial phase of a limited food supply, we ate very well," Loretta said. "We learned to hull black walnuts, and I made lots of goodies with them."

When there was an ice storm back in the hollow, the heavy laden trees fell beneath the weight. As a resourceful man and wanting to use everything God had given him on the land, Arnold cut the trees into firewood.

Arnold could not drive the Bronco up the 50-foot incline from the trail where they had originally parked their camper. The whole area was covered with ice and snow, but he tried it once. He got it all the way to the top and parked it next to the cabin. "We stood inside the cabin and watched it slide back down the ice-covered yard. If we wanted to go anywhere, we had to tie a rope to our back door and slide down the hill to the Bronco."

For the most part, they stayed in the cabin until the ice thawed, but Arnold wasn't very good at staying inside. He'd flatten a cardboard box, place it on top of their drive, and slide down the hill on it. Loretta thought it looked like fun, so she decided to take a turn.

Later, when grandchildren visited, Arnold attached a rope at the top of the slope and let the children hold onto the rope and slide down. They held the rope and crawled back to the top to slide down again. "Oh, my," she said, "what fun we had."

Another reason they enjoyed the snow was because they could have snow cream. They scooped off the top of the snow and mixed it with vanilla, sugar, and eggs.

They were never bored because there was too much to do. They created their own fun and entertainment. They didn't have a television, phone, or newspaper, so Loretta read a lot while Arnold painted.

"It was very quiet on the mountain," Loretta said, remembering one night of excitement. "It was the first night we moved our regular bed into the newly-finished bedroom of the cabin. Believe me, this is not a stretch of my imagination. I witnessed it. When we lived in the camper, mice came in at night. Arnold talked to them, and they would sit up and listen."

Loretta was amazed at Arnold's control over the mice. She, however, intended to keep them at a distance. "We went to bed that night on nice clean linens. Just as we were drifting off to sleep, Arnold moved his leg and raked his toenail across my leg.

I thought it was a mouse and flew right on top of him, screaming for him to get it out."

"Get what out?" he asked, startled and gasping for breath.

"Get that mouse out of the bed."

"I would if you'd get off me so I could get up."

Arnold got up and shook all the bedclothes. He proved to Loretta that there were no mice in the bed. They finally got settled down again and went to sleep, but Arnold never let her forget that night."

6

A Closer Walk with God

Arnold always had faith and confidence that his dream to be a successful painter would come true, that he would realize all that God intended for him. His faith gave Loretta and him strength to live each day with excitement, to look forward to what was going to happen the next day.

He'd often claim one of his favorite passages. "He gives strength to the weary and increases the power of the weak. Even youths grow tired and weary, and young men stumble and fall; but those who hope in the Lord will renew their strength. They will soar on wings like eagles; they will run and not grow weary, they will walk and not be faint" (Isaiah 40:29-31, NIV).

Every day, Arnold would jump out of bed before the sun rose over the trees, excited with what the new day would bring into his life. He'd walk outside and look across the mountain to the tops of the trees that reached toward heaven. Even the trees, it seemed to Arnold, wanted to draw closer to God. Arnold couldn't imagine starting a day without God, spending time alone with Him. "Lord, this is Your day. Use me to be everything You want me to be this day."

After Arnold ate breakfast, he climbed into his Bronco and drove to Gatlinburg. He spent the day airbrushing, painting anything delicate or otherwise with an air gun, using his God-given talent to create.

"He also had many opportunities to witness to people," Loretta said, "and he did just that."

One day, Arnold met a man who'd just left his family. He talked to him for quite a while, reading him verses from the Bible and encouraging him. When the man left, he went back to his family, promising Arnold he'd get his life straight.

Arnold believed one of the reasons God led him into full-time painting was to tell others about Jesus. He tried to seize every opportunity to tell them that Jesus died for their sins. He wanted them to know that if they repented and asked Jesus to forgive them of their sins, He would forgive them and come live in their hearts. He wanted them to know that only through Christ could they have eternal life.

Arnold would return home at the end of the day, and he and Loretta would take long walks while he shared the things God was teaching him. Added to his joy was the fact that God used Loretta at the same time. After she'd taken a job at the nursing home, she'd tell him how God allowed her to minister to others as she worked as a Medicaid, Medicare, and private billing clerk.

But then, the time came when she had to walk alone. Arnold started working ten to seventeen hours a day. He loved it, and the people loved it. Although he and Loretta were thrilled that God was using him in such an exciting way, they were spending less and less time together. She was in bed asleep when he came home at night, and he was still in bed when she left the next morning.

It didn't take them long to realize that this lifestyle was not what they wanted, nor what God wanted for them. He had brought them together to encourage each other and to worship together.

About a year later, Loretta gave her notice at her job. They offered her a position of traveling throughout the state, teaching others, and making more money. It would help them get ahead financially, but Arnold told her God had sent them to the mountains, and He would provide. He didn't believe God took them there to separate them or to leave them without the means to live.

Arnold was not surprised when Loretta agreed with him, telling him she had already decided not to take the job. He told her God would bless them and take care of them. "Although we don't see how it's going to work out, we just have to trust the Lord," Arnold told her.

It seemed Arnold became immediately known throughout the area as the grandfather of airbrush. He taught every young person who wanted to learn. A young man named Gary Daniels became his protégé and he learned everything he could from Arnold.

For the first time in a long while, Arnold and Loretta once again took long walks on the mountain they both loved. They also worked with the young people in their church, while seeking God's help for each day.

Arnold took time off from painting to spend time with family and friends. For instance, Bill and Faye Luper, their close friends, visited them for long periods of time. Their children had grown up together. Bill was retired, making it possible for the four friends to go down the rapids in North Carolina every year.

Regardless of where Arnold went, he saw God's beautiful paintings across the earth. He could see God's handiwork everywhere. "As we drove south on I-40 toward the two tunnels over Cherokee National Forest," Loretta said, "he could hardly contain his excitement at the beauty of God's creation that literally filled the earth around us."

An inexperienced mountain driver senses fear and danger maneuvering the sharp curves that come one after another for a short distance. But Arnold saw it as God's grandeur.

"It seems we're going into them," Arnold always said as Cherokee Mountain rose high before them, about forty miles from Ashville, North Carolina.

"Just then," Loretta said, "the road turned, and we drove by the side of the mountain. As we passed the center of the mountain, the trees were spread high on both sides, and we would turn on the curvaceous road. The trees loomed before us, briefly cutting off our view of the mountain. Moments later, we'd exit the forest, and the mountains would spread before us again. Oh, what a thrill it was, and Arnold's excitement grew. Our road trips filled him with such awe that he could hardly wait to return home and pull out his own paint brushes."

When friends came to visit, it was a time of joy, of good times, even as he worked. During one of Bill and Faye's trips, Bill helped Arnold cut down more trees. He took the trees to the sawmill and had them prepared for building a front porch.

"As was Arnold's nature," Loretta said, "he just did things, so he drew up the plans for the porch and started building it. Bill, however, wanted to read and study everything before he drove a nail. So Arnold was driving nails while Bill was reading the plans. Faye and I stood back and laughed. But in a few days we had a porch."

(It was a sad time when they had to say a final goodbye to Faye. It was 1995, and Arnold and Loretta felt the emptiness of losing her. She had been such a help and supporter of what they were doing, and she had blessed them with her love.)

Arnold built a storage room on the back of the cabin, more like a lean-to during prairie days. They did not have enough money to put a regular roof on it, so he covered it with a polyester one. The polyester roof consisted of long strips purchased in various sizes that could also be used as insulation on a roof or on a temporary room, such as a roof on a green-house. However, he accomplished his goal. The polyester roof kept everything inside dry.

Early one morning, he went outside and saw coals coming down from their chimney and landing on the roof of the storage room. The coals had set the roof on fire. He screamed for Loretta to get outside.

"The roof's on fire," he called to her.

"We no longer had a storage room, and our make-shift chimney could not be used again," Loretta said. "God, however, supplied our needs. Through our church, He provided help to replace our chimney. It was very cold at this time."

Two years after they settled in their little cabin, their youngest daughter came up to visit and decided to stay for a while. She soon met a young man. They fell in love and married about a year later. Several friends and family members came up for their wedding. Everyone stayed in campers, tents, or in the small cabin.

"Oh, what fun!" Loretta said. "What an experience!"

Loretta had another reason to celebrate. "My mother and father finally came up to see us," she said. "Nothing could keep them from their granddaughter's wedding. By then, we had a bathroom, and my mother really enjoyed herself. As a matter of fact, after that, she came up almost every year until she couldn't travel."

They had some good times during the cold, icy, snowy weather. While Arnold painted and created mentally all the things he wanted to do, Loretta had time to read.

Every year, usually in the spring after a winter of snow and ice, a tile on the hollow road washed out. Arnold and Loretta could not get in or out of the hollow. The county spent a lot of money replacing the tile. However, as an engineer, Arnold was knowledgeable of road work and suggested how they could replace the tile so it would not wash out again. They finally accepted his suggestion. "As far as I know, a tile on the road has not washed out again," Loretta said.

During the winter months, off-season for tourists, Arnold did not have work in Gatlinburg. So the income they made in the summer and fall had to last until the next spring. But they never went hungry or cold.

They learned to be still and know God. "That wasn't too hard for Arnold as he was very patient and longsuffering, but I'm impatient and want to rush things. We had the young people up a lot during those months and had parties and games."

Of course, Arnold and Loretta's dream was to build a house on top of their mountain. That involved a lot of preparation, and in the meantime, they saved whatever extra money they had and waited on the Lord.

Since they enjoyed sliding down the hill on a piece of cardboard, Arnold decided to build a sled. Their rides were enhanced as they rode across the snow-covered mountain in a sled they could guide.

He enjoyed taking people to the top of the mountain in their Bronco. That was the only way they could ride up because there were no roads, just paths. It was a joy ride for them, but some people came back saying they'd never do that again. "He just laughed," Loretta said.

After the cold hard freezes of winter, spring came with all its glory. "It is a beautiful time on the mountain. We went outside every morning and looked at the dogwood, redbud trees, and mountain laurel growing wild around us. The mountainsides were full of the beautiful plants, and the strong, delicious fragrance filled our nostrils. All we could see was God's beauty, and we praised Him for it. We truly learned to live."

In April, with winter over, Arnold went back to work. Loretta spent hours and hours alone. She did not want to take a full-time job because her mother became seriously ill, and she didn't know when she would be called back to Florida.

"I discovered that many older people could use my help," Loretta said. "I drove them to various places to take care of their business, ran errands for them, helped with the sick, and sat with them. Many times I made homemade pie crusts and put in their freezers. Most of our neighbors and friends out of the hollow had gardens and grew more than they could use. They kept us supplied with fresh vegetables. I froze them, and that's what helped us through the winter months as well."

7

Making Straight the Way

Arnold worked tirelessly on their property during the tourist off-season and when weather permitted. He cleared a large flat area on top of the mountain for their house and yard. The property had never been lived on before.

"It seemed nature rebelled against our modernizing it," Loretta said.

They could not drive up the mountain, so they walked up an old trail to the top. One day as they walked up, Arnold decided they needed a place to rest. Halfway up, he sliced a large log and used concrete blocks for legs. He put the flat side of the log up so they had a nice bench to sit on and rest.

"Sometimes we spent hours sitting on that bench," Loretta said, "just gazing at God's handiwork. We always thanked Him for all He had done for us."

They carried their groceries and other things up by hand. They didn't mind. They had been walking the trails on the mountain for a long time.

Through all of this, Arnold never lost faith and assurance that one day their permanent home would be completed and they could move out of the hollow. With his endurance and faith in the Lord, nothing could stop him. Even when he couldn't drive to the top of the mountain, he took his walking stick, their Bovea dog, and walked up the drive two or three times a day.

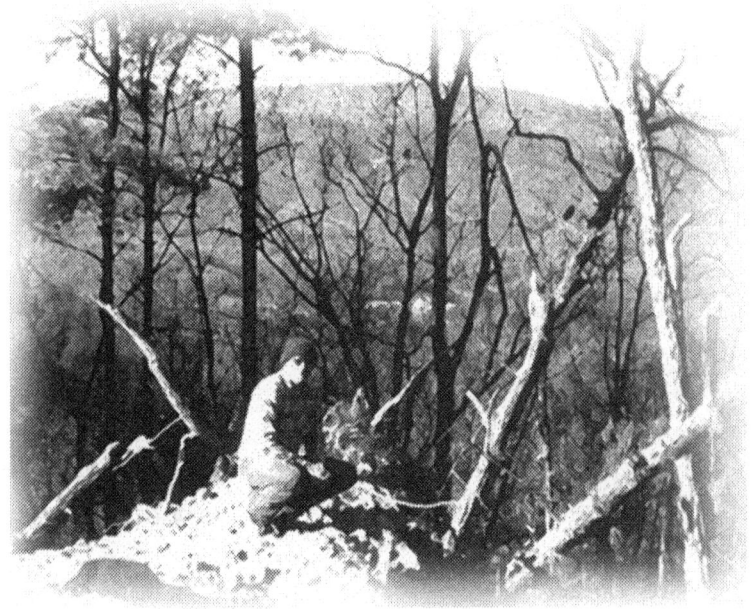

Arnold and his dog taking a break from climbing the mountain.

From 1982 until 1983, Arnold and Loretta spent all the money they had saved for a drive leading to the site of their permanent home. In 1983, Arnold hired a man to bulldoze the drive that abutted their temporary cabin at the bottom of their mountain and led to their property at the top. That was quite an ordeal because it was a 90-degree angle with a slingback, an extremely steep curve.

The dozer driver said following the old trail was the only way to build the drive. Arnold disagreed. He wanted to make a couple of curves going up, making the drive up much easier.

"He was a civil engineer technician and knew what he was talking about," Loretta said. "However, the driver did not think he could do that. As usual, Arnold did not argue with him. He was too easygoing. Therefore, we still had an enormously steep drive.

"Oh, but what a joyous day," Loretta said, "when Arnold and I drove the Bronco up the drive for the first time. However, only vehicles with 4-wheel drive could maneuver the rough, steep hill."

Later, in 1983, Arnold hired a construction company to build a basement for their permanent home at the top of the mountain. They dug out the basement and put tar paper all around the edges, then placed concrete blocks, one row, twelve blocks high around the inside edge of the basement.

In the evenings, when Arnold came home from work, he would go up the mountain and put steel posts down the middle of each column of blocks. He would mix concrete and pour it into every block, making the walls solid.

"When he finished," Loretta said, "everyone said the basement would never move because he made it storm proof. By now, Arnold and I were excited. It looked like we might get the house built one day."

In 1984, they spent every penny they had to buy building materials for their permanent home. "And being the lackey I was for him, I went everywhere buying all we needed. I also bought his art supplies. He called me his gofer. Of course, he worked day and night to make us a living. Also, he would stay up late at night drawing plans for our house. The next day he'd ask if I wanted to change or add anything."

During this time, with their neighbors and Arnold's nephew's help, they began the construction of their permanent home. Loretta learned to drive nails and sand doors, window-sills, molding, and kitchen cabinets. She learned how to put polyurethane finish on the wood made from the lumber from the trees they cut down on their property.

Arnold's nephew built the kitchen cabinets, door facings, baseboards, and doorframes out of poplar, which is hardwood. "Some of the boards were so wide we didn't have to use but one piece to build our cabinets and kitchen closets," Loretta said. "Our neighbors cut the boards, and we had it kiln dried in Gatlinburg. For a city girl, I learned a lot."

8

A Time of Sorrow

In March 1985, sickness and death hovered over them when Loretta received a disturbing phone call. "My sister called and said it looked like my mother wasn't going to make it much longer. She had a bad heart and melanoma cancer. I went to Jacksonville the first of April and stayed with her for two weeks before she went home to be with the Lord. She was 65 years old in March and died in April.

"It was hard for Arnold and me because she was waiting to see us in our permanent home. She talked about it a lot. She visited us often while we were in the cabin because she liked it so much on the mountain. She always said, though, that she just wanted to see us in a real house.

"She truly loved her son-in-law," Loretta said, "and she didn't make any beans about it. Of course, he loved her as well."

"Mama Dill," he'd say, putting his arm around her if she was upset. "I love you, and Jesus loves you."

"She would smile," Loretta said, "and forget all about what she was upset about. Without realizing it, Arnold had rejuvenated her memories of the past."

The history of her and Arnold's families is engrained in Loretta's heart. "His grandparents had lived a mile down the road from Mama's parents, so Mama had known and loved his family since childhood. Mama and I lived with my grandparents when I was a little girl, and our families remained close through the years. I knew his grandparents as Uncle Wesley and Aunt Annie Stanfield, and his uncle Adolph Stanfield was our pastor at Old Rich Baptist church."

Loretta was too young to remember all the details, but the stories of the lives of the two families were passed on to her.

> When Arnold's parents married, they left the farm and moved to Brunswick, Georgia. During his childhood and youth, however, he spent summers with his grandparents. I've been told that his grandfather walked miles down that old dirt road every Sunday to open the church doors. No doubt, Arnold often walked along beside him during those hot months. Every Sunday he watched and listened to his grandfather lead the church in singing.

> Farm work kept our families apart during the summers, so Mama did not remember meeting Arnold until he and I started dating. As a grown man, he reminded her of the way life had been so many years before when his grandfather lived.

> She loved to hear him pray because she said he sounded so much like his grandfather. No wonder my mother loved him so. I don't remember Arnold when we were growing up, but after we were married, he sometimes teased me about those years.

"I remember you, Loretta," Arnold would say with a twinkle in his eye. "I used to pull your ponytails."

"Arnold and I marveled at how God worked in our lives, knowing He led us from the farm and entwined our lives years later," she said, her own fond memories fresh in her heart.

Later, Loretta took a full-time job with the shop where Arnold worked. Arnold and Loretta rode to work together, delighted they could spend more time with each other.

Soon, though, because Arnold had such long hours, Loretta started driving herself into Gatlinburg. Arnold continued to airbrush, but he also painted on the side, using both art mediums in his work.

9

Home at Last

Arnold and Loretta moved into their beautiful permanent home on top of the mountain in September, 1985. With their move, they were no longer in the hollow.

"The day we moved in," Loretta said, "we knelt in the yard and thanked God and praised Him for our Blue Heaven. That's what we called it because we had stained the outside of our home a country blue."

That day, when the trucks started up the drive to deliver our new living room suit, they got caught in the big curve and could not get to the top of the mountain. "I went out and guided them to the top, just like Arnold told me to do. Later, a UPS driver could not maneuver the climb up the mountain, but he was afraid to back down the drive. Arnold went down with our four-wheel drive and pulled him to the top."

Their vision of the home God allowed them to build on the mountain had come true. "Oh, how we continually praised the Lord for our new home. We had so much room we didn't know what to do with it. All our sacrifices and hard work were worth it all to live in our permanent home. However, another part of our dream had not yet come true," Loretta said, referring to the steep drive up the mountain.

Finally, though, they turned their attention back to the drive and covered it with rock. After that, a vehicle without 4-wheel drive could make it up the mountain unless there was a large amount of ice and snow. Still, when it was raining or snowing, Loretta did not try to drive up, but Arnold did.

In October, 1985, a month after they moved into their permanent home, Arnold and Loretta decided that Arnold should give up airbrushing and freelance painting in Gatlinburg and Pigeon Forge. It was time for him to concentrate on his painting. He wanted his own shop in a wide-open space where he could work freely and full-time with the fine arts.

10

Blazing Through the Nineties

In 1991, Arnold rented a three-room building on Highway 321 in Cosby and opened Stanfield Art Gallery. A year later, he turned one room into the art shop he'd dreamed of for so long.

Soon afterwards, an excruciating pain restricted the use of his legs, and it was difficult for him to sit and paint. Finally, with intense pain searing his legs, he consented to have his varicose veins removed. His recovery time was short, and soon he was back at his easel.

One day, as he prepared to work on his truck, as he always kept their vehicles repaired, he placed logs behind the back tires to keep the truck from rolling. With his work finished, he removed the logs. To his surprise, the truck started rolling. He jumped on the running board and stuck his head through the open window to reach the gears. His head hit on the inside of the metal door jam, making it impossible for him to grasp the gear shift. The truck went over the cliff, his head halfway through the window, partially decapitated.

He held the scalp of his head in place as he slowly crawled up the side of the mountain. From the house phone, he called 911.

He also called a neighbor who had to guide the rescue squad up the mountain. His injury required more than a hundred stitches, and he had to sit and sleep in a recliner for six to eight weeks.

"It was a miracle he lived," Loretta said. "Of course, he could not paint during this time, and my heart broke each day when I had to leave him and drive into Gatlinburg to work."

Although Arnold trusted God completely, sometimes discouragement settled over him. Then he remembered Jeremiah 10:23-24, knowing God had led him to the mountain and into full-time art. God had shown him in so many ways that this was His plan for him.

"Show me now, again, Lord, and correct me in all my plans," he prayed, "and anything I have done, if I have stepped off the path of Your will. It is not for me to direct my steps. Show me Your way, oh, Lord."

The Lord encouraged Arnold, and from his studio, he refined his painting. His excitement grew as God continued to fulfill his dreams.

In 1992, he started the official art school in the gallery for the local children. The school was a great success, and the young boys who signed up were enthusiastic and eager to learn. Arnold was perceptive of the needs around him, and as a result, took one young boy under his wing and mentored him. He invested hours of his time, teaching and guiding many boys and girls and several women who took his art classes.

David Popiel, editor and co-publisher of the *Newport Plain Talk*, Cosby, Tennessee, remembers Arnold's contribution to the community.

Arnold Stanfield was busy helping youngsters to learn facets about arts and crafts when I first met him and photographed the occasion many years ago. What amazed me about his talent was the variety of media in which he worked. He obviously loved nature, as he often depicted wildlife in its natural freedom.

The true breath of his talent can be seen in his murals that are in many places, such as the one he did not far from his home at Cosby. It was a moonshine still and operator painted on the walls of a bank vault no longer in use as a bank but as a community center. He did it as a contribution to the community and that showed he wanted his art to be shared and seen. _____ David Popiel

Arnold felt God had not only gifted him with the ability to paint, but had enabled him with the proficiency to help others. "One of his first opportunities came," Loretta said, "soon after he started art classes. He taught Girl Scout groups how to airbrush their troop numbers, flowers, and names on T-shirts and other objects. For some Girl Scout groups, he painted the girls' logo and Ramps Wild Onions on pots."

Arnold taught Scout groups how to make airbrush signs. They placed these signs in the surrounding areas to advertise the different festivals they were in. The girls, in turn, invited him to their functions.

"Throughout the 1990's, he taught many art classes," Loretta said. "At the end of the courses—some ran for one or two years—graduation ceremonies were held, and Arnold presented certificates to students." Even with his busy schedule, Arnold taught eager minds to use the skill of painting that God had also ingrained in them.

These young artists produced oil paintings which showcased their artistic skills and proclaimed the unselfish love their instructor had in developing creative talents among his protégés.

He never tired of helping potential art students work toward their dreams of painting. He was particular in his teaching and made sure students conquered basic lessons on the techniques and perspectives of art. Many of them learned the craft of working with applewood art.

Every time Arnold finished a phase of work with the students, David Popiel, would go to the gallery and take pictures for a newspaper article. The publicity encouraged art students in Arnold's classes, and they worked even harder.

"He not only taught them art," Loretta said, "but integrity and love for their fellow men. He was different from a lot of artists as he never tried to keep anything to himself that he had learned. He always wanted to share all of his work."

Arnold helped others in whatever way he could. For instance, soon after Arnold opened his art gallery, he set up the third room of the building so he could help his fellow artists by selling their works. Loretta worked in the gallery with Arnold and two other employees. "In addition to the paintings, crafts such as quilts made by women in the area and Smoky Mountain wood crafts were sold."

As early as 1990, Arnold had perfected his painting, and his name and craft were known throughout the area. As Arnold blazed into and through the 1990's, his heart soared as on eagles' wings. It seemed that God stamped everything he did with approval. Arnold knew that all he did was a gift from God, and he made sure he honored Him with his talent.

During the next few years, his art created a trail of history in the mountain area he loved. He did his first pencil sketches in 1990 and 91. With his pencil, he meticulously laid every brick and stone. "As an engineer, he could not just draw them to look like bricks and stones," Loretta said.

"His personality added nostalgia to every sketch. I think even he was surprised at how well the sketches turned out."

At that time, the Old Train buffs came in once a year from Ashville, North Carolina. He'd go down to Train Day in Newport and sell his prints.

The following drawings were Arnold's first pencil drawings.

Arnold did many pencil sketches, but the ones he especially treasured were his historic Cocke County scenes:

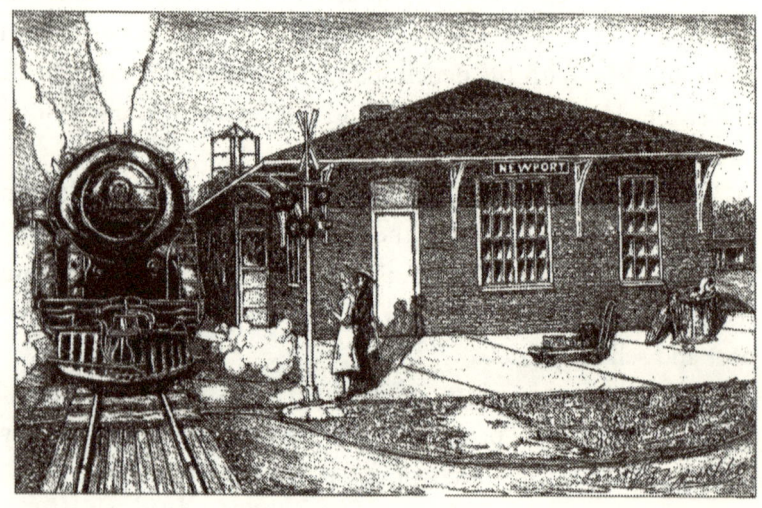

Oops O'Grady—Newport Depot

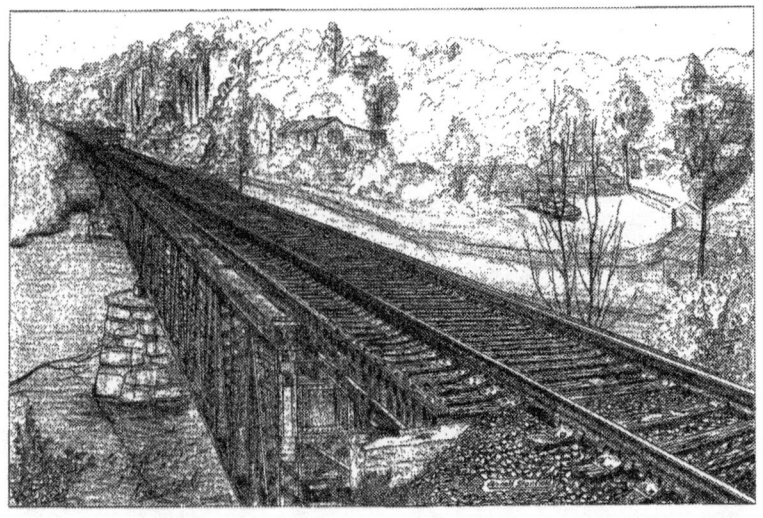

Tracks—Train Tracks in Newport

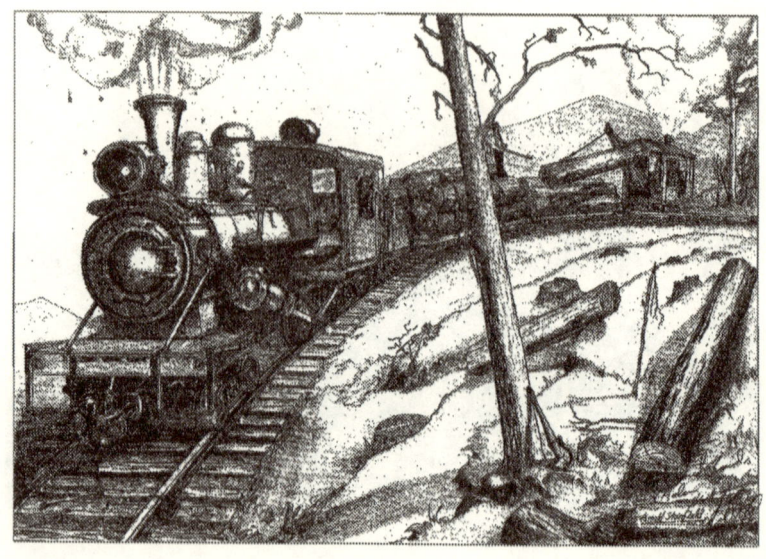

Shay On The Mountain—Logging Train in Mountains

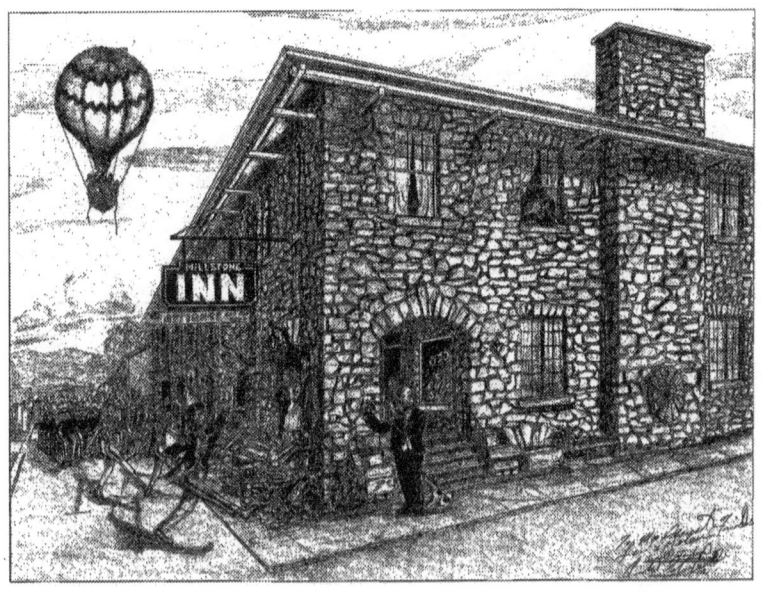

Leader Of The Band—Mill Stone Inn in Newport, TN

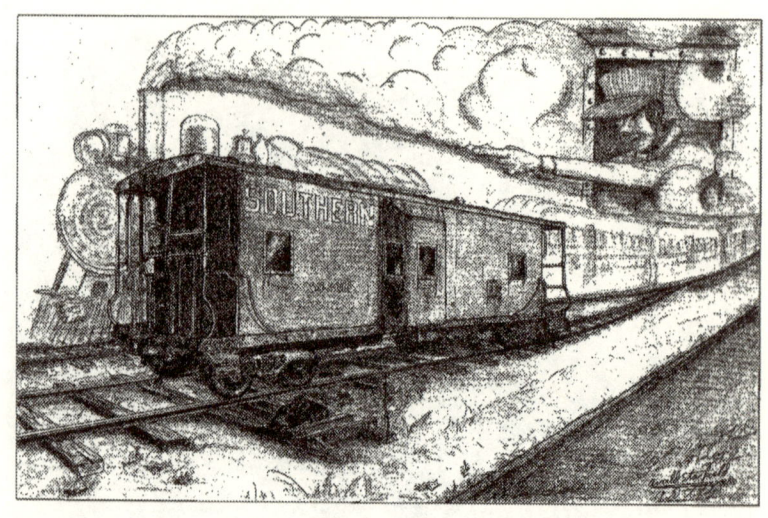

Whata Switch—Southern Rail Car in Newport, TN

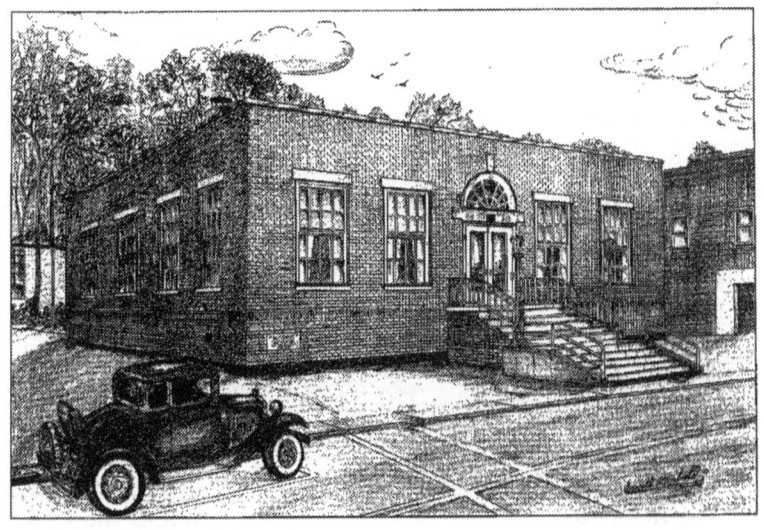

Driving Miss Myrtle—Old Post Office in Newport, TN

As early as August, 1992, Arnold wrote his own advertisements for the Stanfield Art Gallery. He promoted his different types of work, such as oils, acrylics, drawings, renderings, and lessons. In some of his advertisements in the *Newport Plain Talk*, he highlighted his applewood art and other mediums. Regardless of Arnold's project at hand, he continually gave God the credit and praised Him for all He had allowed him to do.

Arnold's work was seen in 1991 by the Walker family whose ancestors had lived in the Cades Cove area of the Smoky Mountains. The region is just outside of Gatlinburg and off the highway that leads to Cherokee. The Walkers were the last family to live in the area on the way to Cades Cove before the government took it over and made it a national park.

The descendants of the Walkers who had lived in the Cades Cove area came to Arnold's gallery in Cosby and commissioned him to paint several portraits of the original Walker cabin. The Walker cabin is still intact and has become a part of the national park.

Then the Walkers commissioned Arnold to create some paintings from old photographs in newspaper articles. "After Arnold completed the paintings," Loretta said, "the Walkers brought a 90-year-old relative to see them. They were all thrilled with Arnold's work."

Every time Arnold received a request from the Humane Society to create a piece of work, he donated it into fund-raising for them. When they sold one of his prints, they could keep the proceeds. Furthermore, any organization that asked him for a special painting received that piece of art for a donation to that organization. He wanted people to become keenly aware of the magic of art and the gift God had given him so they could understand that God could also use them through whatever gifts He had given them.

Many businesses, such as the Stokley Memorial Library, local motels, and Chamber of Commerce requested his work. Even today, his art is still displayed in these and numerous other locations.

Arnold was finally doing what he felt God had called him to do. As a result, residents throughout the county requested his art work. Individuals asked him to paint everything from boat numbers on their boats to painting a grandmother in her chicken yard.

In Peggy Rice's feature article and photo in the *Newport Plain Talk*, Arnold is shown working as he creates a painting of the Cosby Missionary Baptist Church. In the same tribute, he is shown with his painting of Ken Lane's grandmother, Julie, surrounded by her chickens. "He took an old black and white photograph and produced an oil painting from it," Rice said.[1]

"Arnold was commissioned to paint a portrait of the Cosby church," Loretta said, "as well as directional and denominational signs. He also included the preacher's name, the name of the church, and a picture of the church on the sign."

About the same time, the congregation at Union Missionary Baptist Church, the church Arnold and Loretta joined in April, 1980, commissioned him to paint a portrait of Christ. "Arnold felt honored at the request," Loretta said. "It was a time of excitement for him to be able to portray what Christ meant to him. I was in awe that he could paint what he did from his heart with nothing to go by except his relationship with Christ. It was a beautiful experience for Arnold and me. The painting still hangs behind the podium."

David Popiel's photo of Arnold's painting of Christ appeared in the *Newport Plain Talk*.[2] "Sometimes I show my small color painting to friends and share with them my memories of the times Arnold and I served together at the church," Loretta said.

Another big moment for Arnold was when he finished the painting of the Bogard School in 1991. "That was a highlight in his career," said Loretta. He was not commissioned to paint the portrait of the school, but from the time they moved up there, he dreamed of painting that school. They would drive by, and he would stop and gaze at the building. "I'm going to paint that building," he'd say.

Then tragedy struck. The school burned, and Arnold was sorry he had waited so long. Not one to give up, he found someone who had several pictures of the building that included students at the school. That was all he needed. From those pictures, the old schoolhouse came alive in his painting.

Arnold actually painted the children's faces, but then he learned it was not permitted. Rather than discard his painting, he painstakingly created fictional individuals and repainted every face in the picture so that not one face resembled anyone.

Arnold joined several organizations to promote art, and one year he was elected president of the Cosby Ruritan Club. "The club commissioned Arnold to paint a picture of the deceased, Mr. Sass Roberts, who was the president of the National Ruritan Club," Loretta said.

"Arnold painted the portrait in 1992," she said, "and we were both present when Mr. Charles Moore, a past president of the Ruritan club, presented the portrait to Mr. Roberts' widow. The event took place at a Ramp Festival, an annual occasion for almost fifty years. Many years ago, the President of the United States would occasionally attend the festival."

Arnold's prominence traveled fast. As he was recognized more and more throughout Cosby, Newport, and surrounding communities, he became a celebrity in his own right.

"Newport officials asked Arnold to paint a rendering of the Pisgah Presbyterian Cemetery on Highway 321 and Broad Street," Loretta said. They wanted to turn the old Indian cemetery into a beautiful memorial park that would honor the lives of those put to rest at the foot of the mountain. Arnold's drawing of the grounds included explanations as to what and who was there. The cemetery was high on a hill, so he put steps going up to it. The burial ground is one of Newport's historical sites in the center of town. "*I* cherish the rendering Arnold did of the cemetery," Loretta said, a touch of nostalgia in her voice.

Locals and visitors driving past the cemetery sense the love Arnold put into the sketch. Many observers walk up the steps to read the names on the stones. As they gaze upon the beauty Arnold captured and the history recorded in the Indian cemetery, a love and respect for times past is real. And that's what Arnold wanted.

Arnold loved the mountain area, especially Cocke County. To show his appreciation to his friends and neighbors for all they did for Loretta and him from the first day they moved into the hollow, he taught classes and encouraged the community to get involved in art.

He enjoyed the challenge when he painted original homes. "About 1993," Loretta said, "he painted a home that had fallen down. He painted it as the woman instructed him, telling him what it looked like before it fell down. After Arnold finished the painting, the woman said it looked exactly like her home place, the place where she grew up."

Not long after that, Arnold felt the excitement of working with applewood. "Danny Ray Carver saw a lot of Arnold's work," Loretta said, "including all the signs he'd had Arnold paint to advertise his apple orchard on Highway 32."

Since Arnold's first painting, Danny has displayed and sold Arnold's work in his heavily-trafficked long, barn-like country store that also has a large restaurant in half of the building. A candy store with many homemade candies and other specialties is across the driveway.

Visitors and locals crowd onto the premises where they can purchase almost anything grown in the area. Canned foods and preserves are throughout the store. The walls of a two-room concession and dining area are covered with Arnold's paintings. The apple orchard reminds Loretta of Arnold's joy and delight when Danny Carver offered him the apple wood. Loretta explained Danny's gift:

> Danny had a whole barn full of old apple trees that had been sawed and made into slabs. He asked Arnold what he could do with it. Although many artists had asked him for the lumber, he told Arnold that his work impressed him more than the work of any he'd seen.
>
> Danny told him he could have all the applewood lumber if he wanted it. Of course, Arnold wanted it. I could see his excitement growing as visions of what he could do with the lumber emerged in his heart and mind. I remember his gratification and humbleness. It was the introduction to Arnold's applewood art.
>
> He studied a slab of wood for weeks before he started bringing to life what he saw in it. Then he would outline the picture he saw, using just enough paint to bring out the

features he saw in the grain of wood. He called this his applewood art.

Before long, Arnold had perfected his new art. Jim Handley gave a perfect description of the applewood and Arnold's work in the *Newport Plain Talk*.

> The twisted and gnarled wood draws the eye to the shapes of animals hidden deep within the grain created by the many growth rings of the winesap applewood.
>
> Bears, wolves, eagles, and owls appear—enriched by the smoke of a Cherokee Indian storyteller's lodge fire.
>
> These images were placed in the wood's grain by nature, but it took the talents of local artist Arnold Stanfield to bring them out in paint so the rest of us can see them.[3]

Arnold wanted to place his art where many people could enjoy seeing how he had used the almost hidden natural images in the wood to create his magnificent work.

Two of Arnold's applewood art pieces were accepted by the state of Tennessee in a special ceremony at the Tennessee Welcome Center at Hartford on Interstate 40. Several dignitaries attended the occasion in which Arnold dedicated the pieces to the state. They are now locked in cases at the center where many people have the opportunity to study Arnold's articulate work.

Arnold painted *No. 1 June '92* on the applewood art piece he named *Brotherhood of the Spirit*. On the second artifact he painted *No. 2 July '92* and named it *Spirit Son*. Both pieces of applewood art are encased in beautiful varnished cases that Arnold made. A huge fireplace in a large rustic room where tourists wander about separates the two remarkable pieces of artifacts.

Although years have passed, each applewood art piece still glows with newness, with awe, emitting a message that God created the world and all that is within it. Arnold believed God used his hands to show the world a small portion of the beauty of His creation. Arnold brought to the forefront some of the beauty found in applewood art—that splendid creation that's so often overlooked.

Laura Munn, the northeast Tennessee regional manager, was a hostess at the tourist center the day Arnold dedicated the applewood artifact pieces to the state for permanent display.

Jackie Rains, the current manager of the center, has worked in the Department of Tourism for 22 years. Mary Ann Leatherwood is another hostess at the center. In speaking of Arnold's paintings, hostess Deane Galbreath expressed her feeling of his art. "I have a 3 X 8 painting. It's priceless."

Arnold loved promoting the arts, and throughout the years, he entered many art shows in Gatlinburg, Pigeon Forge, and nearby communities. "He attended many events," Loretta said, "such as the Eagle Festival at Patriot Park in Pigeon Forge where he entered his eagle paintings."

During his art career, he painted more than twenty wood grain art pieces of wildlife and enjoyed entering them in art shows. "On every piece of his work," Loretta said, "he always put a number one (1) after his name. The number one was his trademark."

He was one of the original members of the Smoky Mountain Artist Guild. The Guild started the Smoky Mountain Winterfest in which Arnold participated. He was also a member of the State of Tennessee Artist Guild.

11

His Many Outlets

"Arnold was talented and creative in all types of art," Loretta said. "I don't remember much he couldn't do if given time, and outlets for his paintings were numerous."

He did many paintings for his and Loretta's church bulletins. The paintings were filed and used when they needed that particular scene and Bible verse for certain Sundays.

"Dan Ford, a local businessman in Cosby, commissioned Arnold to do a rendering for a new addition for his building where he manufactured mud flaps for 18-wheelers. About the same time, Arnold was also commissioned to do a rendering for our church for future buildings," Loretta said.

In 1980, the company appointed to construct the Acosta Bridge in Jacksonville, Florida, commissioned Arnold to paint a rendering of the bridge. The rendering of the aerial tram that runs through Jacksonville, was included in the commission. Both renderings were completed by Arnold that same year.

"He could create anything," Loretta said, "whether it was to carve on glass for truck owners or create a company logo for Danny Cooke in South Carolina."

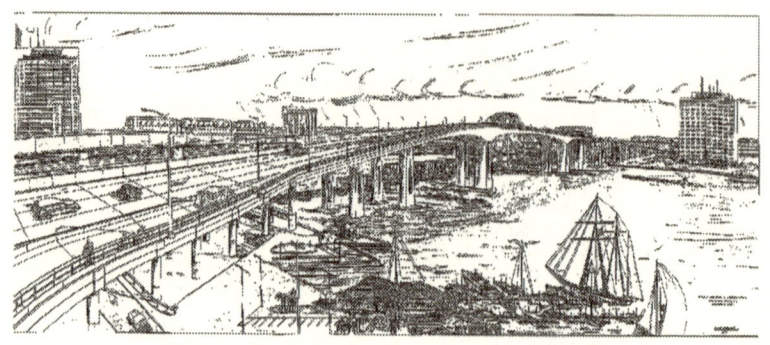

ACOSTA BRIDGE JACKSONVILLE, FLORIDA

Arnold used his ability in many ways. In 1992, he invented several molds for his friend, Tom, who commissioned him to create molds for certain pistols that cowboys, such as Dr. Holliday and other famous gun fighters, used.

"He not only made the molds," Loretta said, "but he poured the pistols, and we both cleaned them up. We made marble, bone, black walnut wood, or other special handles for them. We completed these pistols and numbered each one for the artist who had painted the portraits of the famous gun fighters."

Loretta remembers that it was a real challenge for them to find all the materials they needed to make the handles. "But Arnold knew exactly what we needed. He sent me to a beef butcher in another part of Tennessee who gave us large bones from the cows. I took them home, and he instructed me on what to do. First, I boiled them to remove any meat still on them. Next, I baked them until they dried out. Then Arnold took the dried bones and cut little handles for the guns."

"We'd shine them until they had a special glean, making the handles very pretty," she said. "These were miniature guns, so they were tedious to work with. Still, in one night, we finished enough guns to sell to the art gallery. We made $2,000 that night, and the money was badly needed."

On another occasion, the local high school principal commissioned Arnold to paint a picture of an old hotel that had burned down in 1902 on top of English Mountain, a magnificent pinnacle that borders Cosby, Newport, and the surrounding areas.

The hotel had hot springs in front of it that sprung up out of the earth. It was also the hotel where President Theodore Roosevelt spent most of his vacation time.

Arnold and Loretta went up English Mountain and inter-
viewed the people who lived there. They talked with people
who had shops, trying to find anyone who had a picture of the
hotel. They questioned people for any information they might
have or know about the old hotel.

They located two little pictures about one inch by one inch.
One picture was of the front of the hotel, and the second one of
the back, where the old kitchen was located. Someone had writ-
ten a lot of information on the pictures. With that information
and the pictures, Arnold painted the hotel as it looked before it
burned.

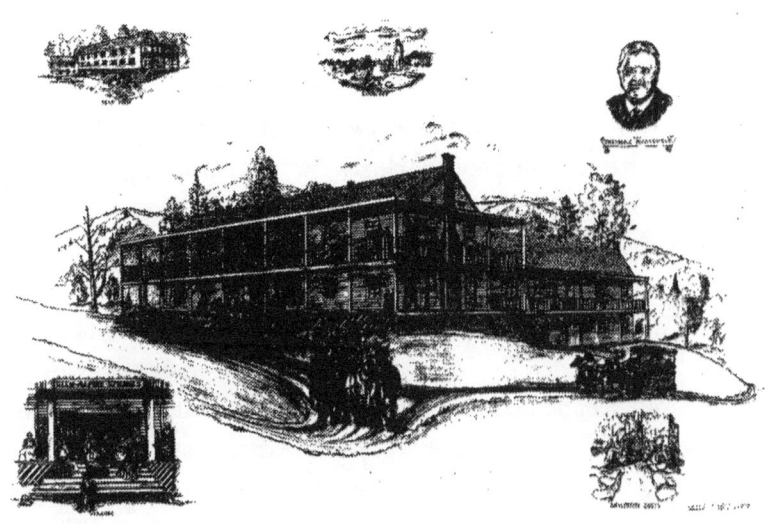

Hotel on top of English Mountain

In those days, the hotel provided a black hack, an enclosed horse-driven buggy, to transport visitors to the hotel all year when the weather permitted. The main attraction to the area was the hot springs and the awe-inspiring beauty that surrounded them. The people who went to the springs believed they were healing springs.

After Arnold completed the hotel painting, he started to create artifacts. Before long, he started making artifacts for other famous artists, such as Terry Redlyn, Beverly Doolittle, and several others.

"Arnold set the artifacts into framed prints, and they turned out beautiful," Loretta said. "When Arnold finally met Bev Doolittle, she told him she knew about him because he had been beautifying her work. He blushed a little. She told him he could beautify her work anytime and that he was doing a good job."

Arnold worked for hours making artifacts. He took paintings that cost $11,000 after they had been framed, and carved things like butterflies, arrows, guns, and other special effects on the frame to match the painting.

Of course, that was widely accepted, so the gallery in Gatlinburg kept a copy of his artifacts and carvings at all times so art buyers could order them to be placed on their paintings.

12

A New Pinnacle

"Arnold closed his art shop in the gallery so he'd have more time and privacy to work," Loretta said. "People loved him and came by just to visit and to see what he was doing. Although he loved for his friends to visit, his work time was limited, and, often, he could not accomplish the work he needed to do.

"He made our garage into his workshop. With his art shop in our garage, he was more in control of visitors and friends just stopping by."

He spent a lot of time in that workshop. As a matter of fact, Loretta would find him down there day and night. "Sometimes at night, I'd wake up and realize he was not in bed. I knew he was in his workshop because that's where he spent some of almost every night. He said that was when he did his best work. Many times, I found him reading his Bible and praying."

During the years of his painting, Arnold became progressively more and more recognized for his work and his creativity. "When he became interested in Indian folklore," Loretta said, "he went to the library and researched extensively, as he did with every subject he painted. He studied Indian history and learned everything he could before he painted the Native American work.

"The more he learned, the more he discovered his love for the culture," Loretta said. "He felt like a little boy again playing cowboys and Indians. So he began his years of painting many Indian scenes and painting a picture within a picture. He named one of his works *Spirit Call #1,2,3,4,* naming each scene respectively, wolf, turkey, deer, and eagle. He found a deep sense of joy and fun as he painted the series of four scenes."

"When he decided to try his carving skills, his first work was to carve a black walnut statue of the wolf, *Spirit Call #1.*"

He later did a carving of an Indian brave and Indian girl at a waterfall. A man saw it in the gallery and kept coming back to study it. One day, he talked Arnold into selling the carving to his wife so she could give it to him for Christmas. "This carving now hangs in the man's home in Newport, Tennessee," Loretta said.

Arnold participated in the Mountains of Chocolate fund-raiser at Mills Auditorium in Gatlinburg. In a photo by Edward Fulford, Arnold was featured on the front page of *The Mountain Press* sampling one of the many chocolate deserts.[4]

"His painting of the wolf received the highest bid of all entrants in the Mountains of Chocolate event," said Loretta. "He donated several pieces of his wolf art to the chocolate show and for different fundraising opportunities for the schools."

In 1998, "the committee for Cosby Tourism asked Arnold to paint a moonshine mural on three walls in the Rhyne-Valentine Cultural Center/First Union Pavilion off Cosby Highway," Loretta said.

The center is also known as the Smoky Mountain Information Center in Cosby. Many activities are held at the center, and the mural is still studied and enjoyed by visitors who stop at the center and those who attend activities there.

"Arnold loved painting the moonshine scene," Loretta said, "because it was the history of Cosby. For instance, Cosby, Tennessee, was the moonshine capital of America for many years. He loved doing anything that pertained to this area of the mountains because it brought him closer to the local people there."

Arnold and Artist Diane Keys, along with others, completed the moonshine display, which features a large metal still that operated years ago in Cocke County. History abounds in this display.

Standing in front of the display, one can see that Arnold used his most keen eye and ability to create the mural as he painted a forest scene, complete with a mountain backdrop. He included revenue agents who stand poised, ready for action, ready it seems, to step out of the painting. A hound dog and a mountain moonshiner are depicted in the true-to-life mural.

A likeness of Arnold's face is almost hidden in the mural. It seemed that Arnold carried his tradition of painting a picture within a painting in the mural as he did with most of his other art work. The moonshine display was dedicated to honor Arnold after his death.

In the fall of 1998, Arnold was commissioned to do 18 murals at the Alamo Steakhouse, a new restaurant in Gatlinburg. The owner was so impressed and pleased with Arnold's work, he asked him to make frames for all the pictures in the Alamo. Arnold finished the work just before the opening in April, 1999. He was present when the Alamo opened its doors to customers.

His brother was the cook, and Arnold helped him and other kitchen employees. Then, he'd run the dishwasher. "No task was too menial for Arnold," Loretta said. "He was never too proud to work at anything as long as it supported us."

The owners of the Alamo told Arnold they would award him the contract for the artwork in all of the Alamo restaurants. The contract would include every Alamo in America and in foreign countries where they planned to build. The murals were of the entire battle of the Alamo and other scenes that took place during the battle.

To add to Arnold's collection of beautiful and meaningful works is his painting of the Sunset Gap Community Center. The Christian center focuses on many aspects of reaching out to the communities, such as teaching, training, and learning.

An original painting of the Gap by Arnold Stanfield was featured in *The Mountain Press*. Beneath the painting are these words:

WELCOME
KNOWLEDGE IS POWER[5]

Arnold captured a part of history in his painting. Tina Alston explained it well in *The Mountain Press:*

> Sunset Gap Community Center has been a focus of its community for decades, providing spiritual and educational support to an isolated society, partly in Sevier County and partly in Cocke County.
>
> The center's history extends back nearly a century when what was then called the Northern Presbyterian Church started a mission school on the county line between Cocke and Sevier counties. Young people from such faraway places as New York and Ohio came to teach and to study the Appalachian culture.[6]

Arnold was commissioned by the board of directors of Sunset Gap to paint a portrait of the center. "He had fun painting it," Loretta said, "as the neighborhood dog wanted to help him. He loved animals, and he thought it appropriate to paint the little black dog into the picture."

Arnold donated more than half of the prints he made of this painting to the Gap. They had bought the original painting but not the rights to it, so Arnold made prints for them to sell for their own profit.

13

Until We Meet Again

Loretta remembers...

As the summer of 1999 passed, Arnold continued to paint and work at the Alamo steakhouse. The owner commissioned him to paint one more mural on the wall of the Alamo. Arnold completed the sketch of the mural he planned to paint on the wall and named it *Joyous Evening.*

On September 16, he came home shortly after midnight, wet and dirty from running the dishwasher. After he came upstairs, he was too tired to eat anything and went straight to bed. The next morning, he said he had severe pain in his left arm. I tried to get him to go to the emergency room, but he refused. I called his doctor, and he said Arnold needed to go to the hospital.

However, Arnold would not go. I talked him into resting most of the day. About two o'clock, he said he felt better and decided to go to work.

On September 18, he awakened with the same pain but much worse. I asked him if he could get himself dressed. He said yes. I got dressed and called the police to have them meet me on the main highway. I was pretty sure Arnold was having a heart attack, and I knew it would take too long for an ambulance to go through the hollow and then drive up our treacherous drive. There was no question that the police sirens would get me to the emergency room faster than I could deal with the traffic.

At the hospital, someone on the medical staff told me Arnold had suffered a light heart attack. There was no heart specialist in Newport, so they decided to med-flight him to the Baptist Hospital in Knoxville, Tennessee. I was told to go home for items we might need before going to Knoxville. They said that once he arrived at the hospital, it would take them a while to get him settled so I could be with him.

Our assistant pastor took me home and then drove me to Knoxville. When I got there, they were performing a heart catheterization on him. Arnold's brother arrived and so did many members of our church family. When they brought him out, he had been joking and cutting up with the doctor and attendants so much, they were all laughing.

The doctor explained that the main artery under his heart was 100 percent blocked. They had put in three stints, and he'd had a light heart attack. However, they said he would be fine, and I could take him home in five to six days. They also said he would be much better in no time.

The doctor told me to wait with my friends in the waiting room until they hooked him up to the heart monitor and several other machines. They promised to call me in and let me sit with him for as long as I wanted.

Thirty minutes later, however, one of the men that waited with me suggested I push the button at the window. It had been much longer than what the doctor said it would take. I pushed the button, hoping someone would come and let me know what was happening.

Just as I sat back down, one of the nurses came out and bent over my chair. I knew immediately something was wrong. He saw the fear in my face and quickly assured me that Arnold was still alive. He hastened to say they were in real trouble but the doctors and nurses were doing everything they could.

As he finished speaking, the heart specialist came out. He shook his head and told me they had done all they could, but Arnold was gone. I was overcome with shock. A little earlier I had been told I could take him home in six days. Thirty five minutes later, he died.

It was almost more than I could cope with. My friends all rushed to me, and the doctor told them to let me get it out of my system any way I could. They were worried because I had already been diagnosed with heart problems.

In a little while, they came and said they would take me into a room where I could sit with Arnold for as long as I wanted. Later, they took me back to the chaplain's office.

The head nurse, who was with Arnold when he died, wanted to talk to me. She asked me if we were Christians, and I told her we were. She said she knew we were because of the way Arnold reacted while he was dying.

"When we told him he was dying," the nurse said, "he started praising the Lord and thanking Him for all He had done for him and for all He had given him. He continued to do this until his last breath."

The nurse said she was so thankful for Arnold's testimony because several of her nurses were not saved. She said she knew they had never experienced anything like that, and she prayed they'd be saved through his witness.

I was thankful Arnold had allowed God full reign of his destiny. As a result, when he left his earthly home, he journeyed homeward praising God for all He had done for him.

Arnold wanted others to answer God's call and to climb the mountain He called them to climb. He knew God would walk with others as He had walked with him.

Although my heart was broken, I experienced the peace of God, knowing Arnold was with the Lord at that very minute. God's Word gave me strength and hope, and as always, I claimed His promises. "I can do everything through him who gives me strength" (Philippians 4:13, NIV).

The shock of it all hit me, our children, family, and friends very hard. He was loved and respected by everyone he met. I can almost hear him reading the words from Job 23:10-12, (NIV).

"But he knows the way that I take; when he has tested me, I will come forth as gold. My feet have closely followed his steps; I have kept to his way without turning aside. I have not departed from the commands of his lips; I have treasured the words of his mouth more than my daily bread."

Epilogue

Memories Live On

Loretta lived on the mountaintop for a year after Arnold's death. She didn't want to leave, but finally, one morning she realized the dangers she faced alone. As she looked out her window across the mountain she and Arnold loved, she saw a black bear saunter across her yard.

Her children wanted her to move back to Jacksonville, Florida, where she would be close to them. It was a harsh decision for her, but she realized it was one she needed to make quickly.

Loretta now lives in Jacksonville, Florida. She attends First Baptist Church where she sings in the choir. She's an outreach leader in her Sunday school class and loves to minister to people. God has filled her heart with love and compassion. Not only does her life honor God, but she honors her husband who taught her the joy of trusting God completely and deeply.

She remembers with warmth and compassion the people in Cosby and Newport, and her neighbors near Short Mountain. "We've never known such dear friends as we had up there," Loretta said. "As a matter of fact, they are still like family to me, and I hear from them all the time. Whenever possible, I still visit the people in the area."

Loretta's grateful for the time she and Arnold lived in the mountains. It's a large area covering many miles, and friends are on every corner. The churches are filled with people from the surrounding area, and they all reach out to show love and compassion to each other.

Memories still fill her heart, and she's filled with energy as she goes from place to place, drawing strength from his paintings she sees everywhere. Down in the right-hand corner, she sees his signature and the date he finished the painting or drawing. She sees the murals he drew, the pictures on the walls, the artifacts.

Her friends are everywhere, remembering her and the precious time they spent with her and Arnold. She glows, remembering the good times she shared with each one.

She said her years with Arnold made her a much stronger and content Christian. "I enjoyed being with him and loving him, and we had such a beautiful relationship. I feel that God sent Arnold here and gave him the talent to paint. God wanted the world to see what He could and would do for those who allowed Him to work through them. I just praise God that he allowed me to be a part of Arnold's life and to see and know what our Savior can do."

In October, 2000, the Mayor of Cosby presented Loretta an award from Vision 21 of Cocke County. The inscription in part, reads "In loving memory of Arnold Stanfield. For all his dedication and contributions to his community and friends."

"Now," Loretta said, "just as I knew they would, the hardships we endured faded away, and only the good times remain."

Tributes

Our Tribute to PaPa
by
Frankie, Tina, and sons, Jason & Steven Proctor

PaPa Arnold won't be sitting on an artist's stool anymore. He won't be telling any more mountain tales to the next generation of grandchildren. He won't be fixing them coffee or starting any fires with them in the old cast iron woodstove. Though his painter's canvas may be empty, our memories today are filled with fondness of him.

PaPa was a quiet man. He liked to be one with nature. It wouldn't occur to him that he was so popular, that he would be missed so much. Yet the day he left our lives, the very fact that so many gathered to celebrate his life says much more about him, and his kindness, than mere words.

PaPa could do almost anything with his mighty strong hands. He could build a house, make a toy shotgun from a piece of wood, paint a perfect portrait of you, fix your car, or rock your tiny baby to sleep.

He loved children and they loved him. This humble man had no trouble at all in conversing with a four-year-old. Children, you see, are the best judges of character. They might not be able to put names on words like decency and honor, but they knew that PaPa was a good man.

In the words of poet Richard Fife:

> No person is ever truly alone.
> Those who live no more,
> Whom we loved,
> Echo still within our thoughts,
> Our words, our hearts.
> And what they did
> And who they were
> Becomes a part of all that we are,
> Forever.[7]

Lovingly Dedicated to my Grandfather

My Papa

by

Stephanie Bailey

Grandfather, the Mighty Eagle has much wisdom, for it follows the footsteps of the old one. Your new Journey takes you beyond the Great Waters. You shall always walk at my side, for in you I have found my way. I have listened to the trees their song has touched my heart. This sacred place among the mountains and clouds shall be filled with your spirit?

Grandfather my heart has cried and my tears are silent as this Sacred Flight. I shall see the Eagle catch his meat and my arrows shall fly in the same winds. Have a safe journey grandfather, for the footsteps you leave I shall follow.[8]

_____Excerpted from Sacred Flight, a poem by Crying Wolf, a Native American.

A Tribute
by
Valerie Nunnery

Any of us as parents know the difficulties associated with raising children, especially teenagers! Arnold became my stepfather at the age of 17, but at the time of his death he was my father in every way. He always had time to listen, would give any of us his last dime, and was a precious grandfather to my children. I have never, nor do I expect to ever, meet a more loving, generous, kind, non-judgmental, and unselfish human being in my life. His loss leaves a great void in our family.

A Tribute
by
Donna Bellamy

Arnold was a very, very special man and we loved him with all of our hearts. He accepted my brother, sister and I as if we were his own children and showed us so much love, even though we were not his. That alone makes him exceptional, as well as so many of his other qualities. We were always amazed by his talents and abilities and loved watching him work. The worst grief my son has ever experienced was when learning of his death, as he was such an important part of his life, and had shown him so much love and attention. I know he is in heaven enjoying the greatest fried chicken and banana sandwiches the never ending, never short of supply banquet table has to offer.

Our Memories of Arnold Stanfield

by

Lt. Colonel Owen B. & Priscilla M. Baker

How pleasant are the memories of Arnold Stanfield. We can only smile and enjoy the thoughts of a wonderful friendship that Arnold gave to us in the years we knew him. He certainly left a legacy of kindness, charity, and contentment with God's will for his life—infusing these traits into all those that had the pleasure of knowing him.

Our first meeting with Arnold came at church. You couldn't miss him, for sure! Tall and distinguished looking, yet quiet and subdued in his personality. He definitely did not have the eccentric nature of most artists. There was a stability and contentment that was infectious in his daily walk and talk. He made you want him as a friend...not a forced friendship, but a desire to know him and spend time with him and his ever so friendly wife, Loretta. (We could say much about Loretta because we still enjoy a wonderful friendship with her.)

Let's get to some specifics. The first time we visited with Arnold and Loretta in their home, we knew they would be life-long friends. They made us feel as welcome as a close family. Arnold did not jump at the chance to show us his artwork and studio. That was not his nature. He did not force anything on you. Instead, there was a desire to know more. Not in a mysterious way, but because you were comfortable around him and always felt at ease. In fact, every time we visited with them, or them with us, we had a hard time ending the visit! We enjoyed their company and always wanted it to last longer.

It was Loretta who suggested Arnold show us his studio and work place. Having an appreciation of craftwork, we could hardly wait. And we were not disappointed! His studio had the typical look of most artists, with paints, brushes, and canvases. But there was much more. His ingenuity was shown in the way he made use of common things in a most uncommon way. Many of his paintings and prints were not just matted and framed, but embellished in very distinctive artwork. For example, he made miniature items and framed them within the matting of the picture itself. Each miniature was made from common household items, such as pieces of a tin can that were fashioned into an Indian spearhead or an antique gun (that looked so realistic that it appeared you could pick it up and shoot it!)

And then here was our discovery of his carving talent! I do not know if Arnold originated the idea or not, but it was certainly new to us when we first saw his carvings in the corner of the wooden picture frame. My, how they added a depth and dimension to the painting itself! The carving always complemented the theme of the artwork, with an attention to detail that made you want to just study the work to find all the things Arnold had put into the carving. And that made you go back to the main painting to see how the carving was an extension of the picture. This was not only superb artwork, but an additional talent that made you appreciate Arnold's artistry even more.

Now, back to the man himself. Several notable character traits come to mind when we think of Arnold. He was an exceptionally kind and thoughtful man. When there was an opportunity to do things for others, he was the trend-setter. It did not matter whether it was helping someone move or volunteering to help at a church cleaning day. Arnold was just as likely to think of something to do for others in a quiet, unassuming way as he was to be part of a group effort for someone else's benefit. He seemed to always think of others first.

Then there was the joy he exuded when helping others! A work day with Arnold became a joyful event. He would joke and point out things in an amusing way, completely overshadowing any difficulty within the work itself. And he always would go the "extra mile" for the benefit of others. Arnold kept you focused on the positive things of life. Hence, our joyful thoughts of every memory of him!

Perhaps the most remarkable memory of Arnold was his contentment with life. He never seemed to question God's plan or purpose for his life. And he certainly trusted God to know what was best for him. Loretta could tell us he was discouraged, but you could not prove it when he was in the public eye! He always had a warm, heartfelt smile and was an encouragement to everyone around him. My, how much better we would all be if we emulated this one character trait alone!

Our fond memories of Arnold are kept fresh every time we look at one of his paintings in our home, especially the one he framed and carved for us. There is no doubt that his life has left an indelible print on many others, too, a most positive print that will stand the test of time. And we have the joy of knowing we will see him again in the Heavenly place that God has prepared for all who have given their lives to Jesus Christ, asked Him to forgive their sins, and have accepted Jesus as Lord and Savior, as Arnold Stanfield did.

Notes

Chapter 10

1. Rice, Peggy. "His love of art has set careers aside." *Newport (TN) Plain Talk,* January 25, 1991, 6d.

2. Popiel, David. Photo. A painting of Christ. *Newport (TN) Plain Talk*, April 5, 1991, 15.

3. Handley, Jim. "Apple wood helps artist make some sweet creations." *Newport (TN) Plain Talk,* May 26, 1993, 16a.

Chapter 12

4. Fulford, Edward. Photo. "Munchie madness." *Sevierville (TN) Mountain Press,* February 2, 1998, 2.

5. Alston, Tina. "Knowledge is Power," Local Christian center continuing decades of work, *Sevierville (TN) Mountain Press,* sec. B, July 4, 1999, 1.

6. Alston, Knowledge is power, 1.

Tributes

7. Fife, Richard. "No Person is Ever Truly Alone." http://www.words-of-sympathy.com/wordsofsympathy/

everyone/103-no-person-is-truly-alone.htm (accessed 3/
13/06)

8. Wolf, Crying. "Silent Flight."
    http://www.indigenouspeople.net/grandfat.htm (accessed
    3/13/06)

978-0-595-39577-4
0-595-39577-5